ANJUM
ANAND

anjum's
INDIAN FOOD

PHOTOGRAPHY BY
VANESSA COURTIER

ALHAMBRA
EDITIONS

EDITORIAL DIRECTOR Anne Furniss
CREATIVE DIRECTOR Helen Lewis
EDITOR Gillian Haslam
DESIGNERS Katherine Keeble, Ros Holder
EDITORIAL ASSISTANT Romilly Morgan
PHOTOGRAPHER Vanessa Courtier
PRODUCTION DIRECTOR Vincent Smith
PRODUCTION CONTROLLER
Leonie Kellman

First published as *Indian Food Made Easy* in
2007 by Quadrille Publishing Limited
This edition first published in 2013 by
Alhambra Editions
Alhambra House
27-31 Charing Cross Road
London WC2H 0LS
www.quadrille.co.uk

Text © 2007, 2013 Anjum Anand
Photography © 2007 Vanessa Courtier
Design and layout ©
    2013 Quadrille Publishing Ltd

Cataloguing in Publication Data: a catalogue
record for this book is available from the
British Library.

ISBN 978 184949 300 0

Printed in China

The unknown can definitely be daunting. I suppose this is why a nation of people who spend as much money as we do on Indian food hasn't yet become adept at cooking it.

But as with many challenges in life, once you climb that hill and face those fears, they were never as tough as you imagined and the rewards can be... well, delicious. At least they are in the case of Indian food! And with the fantastic supply of ingredients now available in the supermarkets or at the touch of a button on the internet, there are no more excuses for not cooking something you love to eat. Indian cuisine seems to be surrounded by an aura of mystery and myths, but the truth is anyone can cook it. And that is the aim of this book – to show you just how quick and simple the recipes can be.

Indian cuisine has always been very straightforward – you cooked what grew locally and along with a helping of bread or rice, that was it. It was and still is a regional and seasonal food that has had spices woven into its very DNA as they are considered the elixir of health. It is, at heart, peasant food, eaten as much for taste as it is for nourishment. Meals traditionally consisted of some protein, a vegetable and a staple. The number of dishes served at any one meal did increase with prosperity which, as many lived in joint families with lots of people there to help in the kitchen, was fine.

However, things have changed and people now have less time to devote to culinary tasks. Indian food has always been an integral part of my diet and long ago I felt the need to simplify, streamline and lighten my meals. I really wanted to bring this fantastic, complex and generous cuisine into the twenty-first century. Food is personal, you cook what you want to eat, so cooking an Indian meal can be as easy as baking some fish, grilling some chicken, stir-frying spinach or rustling up some rice and lentils.

The accepted 'wisdom' that Indian food is unhealthy is an unfair allegation. Indian restaurants are not representative of how Indians eat; we don't add cream, ghee or nut pastes to all of our dishes. This cuisine can seem oily but so can the Mediterranean diet, and I think oil is good, when consumed in moderation. And as the cooked accompaniments that required oil were traditionally served in small portions with either boiled rice or simple bread, you would have needed the oil to stay healthy. Most Indians eat well-balanced, nutritious meals incorporating vegetables, lentils, whole grains, dairy and a little meat or fish – all fresh food and fantastic ingredients. What we see as Indian food in this country is often a murky narration of the truth with much lost in translation. The food is, actually, inherently very healthy.

In the UK, Indian food has been on a journey of evolution. We have moved on from inauthentic creamy, fruity curries and can now easily find tandoori and regional options. But there is still so much to discover. India is a country that has so much to offer. It is food that is eaten for breakfast, lunch and dinner. It is everyday food; food for children, adults, friends and family. But every cuisine has all these elements so why has the obvious escaped us for so long? Why has Indian food been relegated to the upper shelves of book stores – the back bench of the United Nations of Cookery and out of most people's reach for so long?

It has been a long road getting here and a slow but exciting journey, but thankfully we can now experience Indian food the way it was intended, at home.

Anjum

THE INDIAN KITCHEN MADE EASY

You can make Indian food without having to buy any new cooking equipment but if you like cooking Indian food, or in fact any ethnic meal, there are a few bits and pieces that make the experience easier.

NON-STICK KARAHI

No self-respecting healthy eater would be without non-stick cookware. A karahi is a wok-like pan with a rounded base. The curved bottom allows the food to move easily in the pan without bits of food sticking to and burning in the edge. Once you start to use these pans, you never want to go back.

CURVED CAST-IRON PAN (TAVA)

We cook most of our flat breads on this shallow, concave cast-iron pan. The pan holds the heat well and the bread cooks quickly and evenly. If you don't have one, a non-stick frying pan will also get the job done.

GRINDERS, PESTLE AND MORTARS, BLENDERS AND MICROPLANE GRATERS

These are kitchen facilitators. They are not all essentials but I think every self-respecting kitchen should have a blender and microplane grater for making large and small quantities of pastes respectively. Also useful is a pestle and mortar or a small spice grinder for grinding fresh spices.

MUSLIN CLOTH

This thin, light cloth is used when making paneer, traditional Indian cheese (see page 27). It is inexpensive and can be washed and reused.

ROLLING PIN AND TONGS

The rolling pin is essential for rolling out the many Indian flat breads. Tongs are really useful, not only for turning and handling bread but also to turn vegetables and meats that are grilling in the oven.

SPICE CONTAINER

This is a round steel container – not very attractive but really useful. It houses small deep bowls in which you place all your most used spices so that when you are cooking everything you need is to hand. I actually have two – one for powdered spices and one for whole. This means my cupboards are free of plastic bags of half-used and spilling spices.

Lastly, I cook using gas rather than electricity as I find that I have greater control when cooking and that food cooks quicker on gas. I have explained how the dishes should look and smell at the different stages, so follow these guidelines to get the recipe right as well as following the time guide.

THE RECIPES MADE EASY

Whenever I take things for granted or make assumptions, I get into trouble. So, when it comes to cooking a new cuisine, I assume a lack of knowledge and then look forward to learning about it. When it comes to Indian food, I have seen so many people make preventable mistakes (simple things like choosing the wrong chilli or tomato) that have left their dishes less than perfect. It might be useful to have a quick read of this chapter to ensure the dishes turn out as they should and to start to understand the basics. Also have a look at the glossary on page 156. For those of you who have already mastered the basics and are finding cookbooks repetitive, bear with me as we're still in the early stages in this culinary evolution!

CHILLIES

People seem to have forgotten that chillies have a wonderful flavour. They can be really hot to eat but are not spicy as such. Remember the basic rule – the bigger the chilli, the milder it is. Green chillies ripen into red ones but have a slightly different flavour. I find the red ones slightly sweeter than the green ones, a bit like capsicums. I often leave chillies whole in my food so that they impart flavour without too much heat as this is mainly contained in the seeds and membranes.

If you don't have fresh chillies, dried red chillies or even chilli flakes are a good substitute; they add heat as well as a little flavour. Chilli powder, however, will give your food a great colour and lots of heat but little flavour. The important thing to remember is that unless a recipe says otherwise, always use the long, thin green chillies that look like knobbly fingers. Other chillies will not give you the same flavour. If you bite into a harsh chilli, follow with yoghurt or something sweet.

COCONUT

The coastal regions of the south and west of the country tend to use the ubiquitous coconut to sweeten and to add richness and texture to their dishes. I don't always have a fresh coconut at home so often use canned coconut milk and desiccated coconut instead as they work really well. If, however, you love coconut, buy a coconut grater from a well-stocked Indian shop. They are inexpensive, easy to use and it takes just minutes to grate the nut with little effort.

GARLIC

These come in such different sizes, from small and thin to gigantic mutant cloves, so when writing a recipe sometimes indicating how many cloves is not always enough. So, to give you a better indication, one large clove of garlic weighs around 2–2.5g. Yes, I know I'm so pedantic!

GHEE

This is simply clarified butter. It can be bought in stores but is easy to make. Warm unsalted butter in a saucepan and cook gently until the colour changes to pure gold. By this time all the milk impurities will have risen to the surface and should be removed with a spoon. The ghee is now ready to use. Store in a jar in the fridge.

GINGER

People have often asked me where to buy ginger paste, I never realised that people actually bought pastes – they are so easy to make at home. Use a microplane grater or a blender. You can store the paste in teaspoon-sized batches in ice-cube trays in the freezer and add them straight to the pan.

MASALA

I often throw the word 'masala' around, assuming everyone knows what I am talking about. I have now realised that, of course, most don't. It is one of the basic foundations of Indian food. It is, in this context, the mixture of ingredients that forms the base of most curries. It is like making a gravy or curry sauce to which you add the main ingredient. A poorly cooked masala will result in a one-dimensional dish, so take your time and cook the masala properly at each stage. To gauge if it is cooked, look for little bubbles of oil being released on the sides and if still in doubt, try it – if there are no harsh flavours, it is properly cooked.

MEAT AND POULTRY

The best way to get the most from your red or white meat is to cook it on the bone as this provides that wonderful meaty flavour that we often add back in with good-quality stock (which is made from those same bones). We cook our red meat until falling off the bone – there is never any trace of pink – but I leave it to you to cook lamb how you like. If you use meat without the bones, you can either add extra bones to the dish as it cooks and fish them out later, or add some stock instead of water. When cooking lamb, I usually choose shoulder or leg, but you can use cheaper cuts if a recipe requires long, slow cooking. Your butcher will prepare cubed lamb with the bone in if you ask. Also, do skin chicken joints as we do not brown them in the pan and this can leave the cooked skin a little flabby and chewy. It will also act as a barrier, preventing the flavours of the gravy getting into the flesh.

ONIONS

These are a really important ingredient in Indian food. They add depth of flavour, body, richness and sweetness to a dish. Not all curries will have onions, but the onion masala (base of a curry/gravy) will always be used abundantly in north Indian restaurant kitchens. When cooking onions, you need to make sure that the onion is properly cooked and to the right stage. As onions cook, they absorb any oil in the pan, then once cooked they release the oil back and you know they are done. If the recipe says the onions should be soft, then they should be translucent; if golden, then the softened onion should be cooked until browned on the sides and turning golden in the centre. Be wary of cooking the onions over too high a heat when they will brown before they soften – check by pressing a piece.

SPICES

Whole spices should be the first thing added to the hot oil in a pan. They only take 10–20 seconds to cook and when they release their aroma and just start to darken, quickly add the next ingredient. Powdered spices are very delicate so cook over a low heat. Spices should be kept in airtight containers away from heat and sunlight (see page 8). It's always best to buy whole spices as they keep better and retain more flavour. They take seconds to grind in a spice grinder (see page 8).

To roast spices, use a small frying pan or saucepan and dry roast over a moderate to low heat, shaking the pan often to cook them evenly. You can't leave them unattended as they need to be taken off the heat and poured out of the pan as soon as they are roasted and fragrant, around 1 minute. Use a pestle and mortar to grind to a powder.

TAMARIND

This is a coastal fruit that grows in papery brown pods on trees of the same name. It is an important ingredient and is used to add a sour element to many Southern curries. It can be a bit fiddly to extract the paste from the block of tamarind, but ready-made pastes are now available in supermarkets. Add judiciously as they all have different strengths.

TOMATOES

In India tomatoes are used for their slight sourness as well as their flavour. For Indian food, you need to buy the cheap cooking tomatoes – the ones you normally avoid as they look unripe and flavourless. Juicy, sweet plum or vine tomatoes are great for salads and raitas but can sometimes be too sweet for our dishes.

YOGHURT

As yoghurt ages, it gets more and more sour, which is fine as we sometimes need yoghurt for its freshness and other times for its sour quality. Fresh and sweet for desserts and raitas, slightly sour for general cooking and even very sour for some specific dishes; the recipe will always say if it should be particularly fresh or sour. If the yoghurt is too fresh, you may need to add a little lemon juice at the end of the cooking. Taste and decide. The Onken biopot range of yoghurt always seems to work well.

light meals
& SNACKS

succulent
CHICKEN TIKKA WRAPS

MAKES 8

Blend together the ingredients for the marinade and tip into a non-metallic bowl. Pierce the chicken all over with a fork and add to the marinade. Leave to marinate in the fridge for a few hours, if possible. Bring back to room temperature before cooking.

Preheat the grill. Brush the grill rack liberally with oil and place some foil below to catch any drips. Thread the chicken pieces onto the skewers, spacing them apart so they do not touch. Grill for 6 minutes (using the upper shelf if your grill has that option), turning halfway, then baste with the butter and grill for another minute – the chicken should be slightly charred at the edges and cooked through.

Meanwhile, wrap the tortillas in foil and warm in the oven for 5 minutes while the chicken is cooking.

Using a fork, slide the chicken pieces off the skewers onto a plate and sprinkle over the chaat masala, if using. Divide the chicken into eight portions and place each in the middle of a warmed tortilla, top with the vegetables and spoon over 1½–2 tablespoons of the chutney. Fold over the top of the tortilla, pull in the sides and continue wrapping. Cut the wrap in half on the diagonal and serve. Repeat with the remaining tortillas and serve.

500g chicken breast, skinned, boned and cut into 2.5cm cubes
vegetable oil, for frying
10 wooden skewers, soaked in water for 30 minutes
2 tbsp melted butter, to baste
8 tortillas
¾ tsp chaat masala (optional)
½ onion, 2 tomatoes and one head of Little Gem lettuce, all finely sliced
150g coriander and mint chutney

Marinade
150ml Greek-style thick yoghurt
1 tbsp vegetable oil
8g fresh ginger, peeled
15g garlic (approximately 8 large cloves), peeled
¼–½ tsp red chilli powder, or to taste
¾ tsp garam masala
generous pinch of green and black cardamom seeds and fennel seeds, ground together
¾–1 tsp salt, or to taste
30g Cheddar cheese, coarsely grated
1½ tbsp lemon juice
1 egg
2 rounded tbsp gram flour

tandoori
LAMB WRAPS

SERVES 6

Blend all the marinade ingredients until smooth. Pour into a non-metallic bowl, mix in the lamb and leave to marinate for as long as possible – overnight in the fridge would be best. Bring back to room temperature before cooking.

Preheat the grill. Thread the lamb onto the skewers, leaving a space between each piece, and place under the grill. Cook for 5–6 minutes until tender, turning halfway through cooking. Alternatively, cook in an oven preheated to 200°C/400°F/gas mark 6 for 8 minutes. Baste with the butter and cook another minute or two for slightly pink meat (or for slightly longer if you prefer meat well done).

Wrap the tortillas in foil and warm in the oven for the last 5 minutes of the cooking time.

Divide the lamb into six portions and place in the centre of the warmed tortillas. Top with some of the vegetables and spoon over 1½ tablespoons of tangy herby chutney (see page 134). Roll and serve.

These wraps are the perfect grab-and-go meal. You can prepare the ingredients well in advance and simply grill the lamb in the time it takes you to slice the tomato and onion.

400g boned lamb, cut into 2cm cubes and pierced with a fork
10 wooden skewers, soaked in water for 30 minutes
2 tbsp melted butter, for basting
6 tortillas
sliced onions, lettuce and sliced tomatoes, to serve
100ml tangy herby chutney (see page 134) mixed with 3 tbsp yoghurt, to serve

Marinade
150ml Greek-style thick yoghurt
½ small onion, peeled and roughly chopped
15g garlic (approximately 8 large cloves), peeled
8g fresh ginger, peeled
1½ tsp garam masala
1½ tsp ground cumin
1 tsp ground coriander
½ tsp fennel seeds, ground
¼ tsp freshly ground black peppercorns
1 tbsp vegetable oil
2 tbsp fresh coriander leaves
½ tsp red chilli powder, or to taste
2 tsp lemon juice
1 tsp salt, or to taste

paneer, mushroom
& SPINACH WRAPS

SERVES 5

Clean the mushrooms, then boil them in water for 15 minutes. Drain and leave to cool, then slice thickly.

Blend all the marinade ingredients to a smooth paste and tip into a non-metallic bowl. Add the mushrooms to the marinade and leave for 20 minutes.

Preheat the oven to 200°C/400°F/gas mark 6 and oil a roasting tin. Thread the mushrooms, well-coated in the marinade, onto the skewers and bake in the oven for 20 minutes, turning halfway. Once cooked, add to a bowl with the paneer.

Blend all the ingredients for the spinach paste to a smooth paste. Heat the oil in a large non-stick saucepan or frying pan and add the spinach paste and 100ml water. Cook over a moderate heat for about 15–20 minutes or until creamy and you can't taste raw garlic. Add the paneer, mushrooms and onion and cook for another minute or until the onion just starts to wilt.

Meanwhile, wrap the tortillas in foil and warm in the oven for a few minutes. Divide the filling into five portions and wrap each in one of the tortillas. Roll up and cut in half on the diagonal.

Marinade
75ml Greek-style thick yoghurt
¾ tsp each garam masala, ground cumin, fennel
    and green cardamom powder
2 tsp garlic paste
1 rounded tsp ginger paste
2 tsp gram flour
salt, to taste
2 tsp lemon juice
¼–½ tsp red chilli powder, or to taste
2 tsp vegetable oil
2 tbsp water

Spinach paste
225g baby spinach leaves, washed
45g fresh coriander, leaves and stalks
15g garlic (approximately 6 large cloves), peeled
15g fresh ginger, peeled and roughly chopped
6 tbsp roasted and salted peanuts
2–3 tbsp lemon juice, or to taste
1 tbsp vegetable oil
salt and freshly ground black pepper
1–3 green chillies (optional)
200g portobello mushrooms
6 wooden skewers, soaked in water for 30 minutes
300–350g paneer, or to taste (see page 27), cut into
    2.5cm cubes
2 tbsp vegetable oil, for frying, plus extra for oiling pan
100ml water
½ small onion, peeled and thinly sliced
5 flour tortillas

chilli cheese TOAST

MAKES 2

Preheat the oven to 200°C/400°F/ gas mark 6. Mix together all the ingredients except the bread. Pile the mixture evenly on top of the bread and bake in the oven for a couple of minutes until crisp and browning on the sides. Serve hot.

100–120g Cheddar cheese or your preferred cheese, grated
10g onion, finely chopped
½ small tomato, finely chopped
¼ tsp finely sliced green chillies
1 tsp finely chopped fresh coriander
2 slices of bread

masala scambled EGGS

SERVES 1

Heat the oil and butter in a non-stick frying pan. Add the onion and cook for 2 minutes.

Meanwhile, whisk the eggs with the tomato, chilli, fresh coriander and salt. Add the eggs to the pan and scramble as you would normally, leaving them a little longer than usual.

1 tsp vegetable oil
small knob of butter
¼ small onion, peeled and finely chopped
2 eggs
½ small tomato, finely chopped
½ green chilli, finely sliced
1 heaped tbsp chopped fresh coriander
salt, to taste

savoury
SEMOLINA CAKE

SERVES 8

Preheat the oven to 200°C/400°F/gas mark 6 and oil a large 8–9 inch loaf tin.

Mix together the semolina, yoghurt, water, vegetables, ginger, spices and salt to make a batter of a medium-thick consistency. If it is too thick, add a splash of water. Taste and adjust the seasoning if necessary.

Heat the oil in a small saucepan. Add the mustard seeds and cumin and cook on a low flame, until they stop popping. seeds and cook for about 20 seconds until the mustard seeds have popped and the cumin is aromatic. Stir into the batter.

Stir in the bicarbonate of soda and immediately pour the mixture into the prepared tin and sprinkle over the sesame seeds. Bake in the preheated oven for 35–40 minutes. The cake is ready when a toothpick inserted into the centre comes out clean and when the edges are crisp. Leave the cake to cool in the tin.

Use any vegetables you have – either those listed here or experiment with courgettes, cabbage, spinach or fresh fenugreek leaves.

3 tbsp vegetable oil, plus extra for oiling
165g semolina
125ml plain yoghurt
125ml water
40g frozen peas
2 tbsp chopped onion
1 small carrot, peeled and grated
handful of frozen or fresh green beans, roughly broken up
8g fresh ginger, peeled and pounded into a paste
¼–1 tsp red chilli powder, or to taste
½ tsp turmeric
salt, to taste (season well)
1 tsp mustard seeds
½ tsp cumin seeds
¾ tsp bicarbonate of soda
1 tsp sesame seeds

paneer

Bring the milk to a boil in a heavy-based saucepan. Once the milk starts to boil and rise up, stir in 200ml of the yoghurt or all the lemon juice. Keeping the milk on the heat, stir gently to help the milk curdle – it should only take a minute or so. If it does not separate, add the rest of the yoghurt and keep stirring. The curds will coagulate and separate from the watery whey. Remove from the heat.

Line a large sieve with muslin or cheesecloth and place over a large bowl or saucepan. Pour the cheese into the lined sieve and run some cold water through it. Wrap the cheese in the cloth and hang it from the tap over the sink to allow the excess water to drain for 10 minutes. Then, keeping it fairly tightly wrapped, place on your work surface with a heavy weight on top (I refill the same saucepan with the whey or water and place it on top) for 30–40 minutes or until it is flattened into a firm block. Then cut into cubes or crumble, depending how you want to use it.

Store any unused pieces of paneer in the refrigerator in water in a covered container. You can also freeze it in an airtight container. Defrost thoroughly before use.

2 litres full-fat milk
200–250ml fresh yoghurt or
  2 tbsp lemon juice

Paneer is home-made, unsalted white cheese. It has all the taste of a fresh farmer's cheese and a dense, crumbly texture that works wonderfully either combined with the spices of India or served simply with flaky sea salt, freshly ground black pepper and a drizzle of good-quality olive oil.

paneer &
VEGETABLE SKEWERS

Purée all the marinade ingredients until smooth, then place in a non-metallic bowl. Add the paneer and vegetables and allow them to soak up the flavours for 30–40 minutes or longer in the fridge.

Heat the grill to a high setting and oil a roasting tin liberally. Place a roasting tin or some foil below the grill to catch any drips.

Thread the vegetables and paneer alternately onto the skewers. Grill for 7 minutes, drizzle over the melted butter, turn and cook for another 2–4 minutes or until charred at the edges. Alternatively, cook in an oven preheated to 200°C/400°F/gas mark 6 for 8–10 minutes, turning halfway through. Sprinkle the skewers liberally with chaat masala and serve with bread.

This is my vegetarian tandoori recipe. Tandoori food is often served with sliced or chopped tomatoes, red onions and cucumbers seasoned and drizzled in lemon juice, and some tangy herby chutney (see page 134).

300g paneer (see page 27), cut into 2.5cm cubes
1 large onion, peeled and cut into 2.5cm cubes
1 green and 1 red capsicum, cored and cut into 2.5cm cubes
vegetable oil, for greasing
6 wooden skewers, soaked in water for 1 hour
2 tbsp melted butter
chaat masala, to sprinkle

Marinade
125ml Greek-style yoghurt
5g fresh ginger, peeled
10g garlic (approximately 3 large cloves), peeled
salt, to taste
¼–½ tsp chilli powder, or to taste
1 tsp garam masala
2 tbsp lemon juice, or to taste
2 tbsp vegetable oil
1 tbsp gram flour
1 tsp cumin powder
seeds of 6 green cardamom pods, powdered with a pestle and mortar

potato & pea
SAMOSAS

MAKES 20

Heat the oil in a small non-stick saucepan and fry the mustard seeds for about 10 seconds until they splutter. Add the onion and ginger and cook for 2 minutes over a high heat. Add the peas and give the pan a good stir, then add the spices, salt and a splash of water. Cook for 1 minute, then add the potatoes and coriander and cook for 2–3 minutes. Taste and adjust seasoning.

Preheat the oven to 200°C/400°F/gas mark 6. Unroll the pastry, peel off one piece, then cover the remainder with cling film and a damp tea towel to prevent it drying out. Lay the first piece of pastry flat on a clean surface and brush with melted butter. Fold in one third of the pastry lengthways. Brush again with the butter and fold in the other end to make a long triple-layered strip. Halve the strip crosswise – your strip needs to be only about 10cm long.

Place one rounded teaspoon of the filling at one of the short ends of the strip, leaving a 2cm border. Fold the right corner diagonally to the left, enclosing the filling and forming a triangle. Fold again along the upper crease of the triangle. Keep folding this way until you reach the end of the strip. Brush the outer surface with the butter. Place on a baking sheet and cover while you make the rest of the samosas. Before baking, sprinkle with sesame seeds, if using. Bake in the centre of the oven for 30–35 minutes until golden and crisp, turning halfway. Serve with tangy herby chutney or a quick tamarind chutney (see pages 134 and 135).

3 tbsp vegetable oil
½ tsp mustard seeds
60g chopped onion
6g fresh ginger, peeled and finely chopped
60g frozen peas
1 tbsp coriander powder
1 tsp cumin powder
¼ tsp red chilli powder
½–¾ tsp garam masala
1–2 tsp dried mango powder, or to taste
salt, to taste
600g potatoes, boiled until soft, peeled and crushed into large lumps
4 tbsp chopped fresh coriander leaves
1 packet filo pastry
5 tbsp melted butter, for brushing
2 tbsp sesame seeds (optional; you can also use poppy or nigella seeds)

chicken

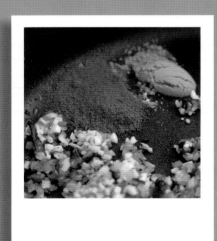

chicken in
CREAMY YOGHURT

SERVES 6–8

Purée the garlic and ginger with some of the yoghurt to make a smooth paste, then stir in the remaining marinade ingredients. Tip into a non-metallic bowl, add the chicken and leave to marinate in the fridge for as long as possible (I leave mine overnight). Bring back to room temperature before cooking.

Pour the chicken and the marinade into a large saucepan and place over a high heat.

Meanwhile, heat the oil in a small pan and fry the onion and chillies, if using, for about 6 minutes or until soft. Once done, add to the chicken along with the cardamom pods and continue cooking over a high heat for about 15–20 minutes until the watery curry becomes creamy and covers only one-third of the chicken.

Cover the pan and cook the chicken over a very low heat for a further 10–15 minutes until it is tender and the gravy is rich and creamy. Stir occasionally, making sure there is enough water in the pan and adding a splash more if necessary. Stir in the coriander, check the seasoning and serve.

1.3kg chicken, skinned and
    jointed into small pieces
2 tbsp vegetable oil
1 small onion, peeled and
    chopped
1–2 green chillies, slit (optional)
1 large or 2 small black
    cardamom pods
handful of fresh coriander stalks
    and leaves, finely chopped

Marinade
15g garlic (approximately 7 large
    cloves), peeled
20g fresh ginger, peeled
400ml plain yoghurt
4 tsp coriander powder
½–1 tsp red chilli powder
1 rounded tsp garam masala
2 tsp salt, or to taste
½ tsp cumin powder

As a bonus for the health-conscious amongst you, very little oil is used in the dish which simply relies on good-quality chicken and fresh yoghurt for its wonderful depth of flavour and creaminess.

goan coconut
CHICKEN CURRY

SERVES 4–6

Dry-roast the coconut in a small pan over a medium heat until it is golden brown. Grind into a fine paste with the red chillies, ginger, garlic, cumin, coriander and poppy seeds. Add a splash of water to help it grind down.

Heat the oil in a non-stick saucepan. Add the onion and fry for 4–5 minutes until it is golden brown. Add the salt and paste and fry for another 5–6 minutes or until all the excess moisture has dried off and the paste has had a few minutes to fry off.

Add the chicken pieces and cook in the paste for 5 minutes over a moderate heat, then stir in the coconut milk and bring to a gentle boil. Turn the heat down to low and cook, covered, for 30–35 minutes or until the chicken is cooked through.

Uncover the pan and stir in the tamarind and creamed coconut; cook for another few minutes or until the gravy is creamy. If there is not enough water in the pan at any time, add a splash or two from the kettle.

Goans often eat their curries with their local bread or red, nutty rice. I think it works well with any rice, naan or even baguette.

6 tbsp desiccated coconut
1–2 fresh large red chillies
8g fresh ginger, peeled
15g garlic (approximately 5 large cloves), peeled
½ tbsp cumin seeds
1 tsp coriander seeds
2 tsp white poppy seeds
1½ tbsp vegetable oil
1 small-medium onion, peeled and sliced
salt, to taste
1kg chicken, skinned and cut into small joints
250ml coconut milk
2 tsp tamarind paste, or to taste
50g creamed coconut

oven-fried
CHILLI CHICKEN

SERVES 6

Blend all the marinade ingredients into a paste and place in a non-metallic bowl. Add the chicken and coat well in the paste. Leave in the fridge to marinate for a couple of hours or overnight. Bring back to room temperature before cooking.

Preheat the oven to 225°C/425°F/gas mark 7. Pour the oil into a roasting tin large enough to accommodate the chicken in one open layer. Place the pan on a high shelf in the oven to heat up for 15 minutes.

Mix the salt, black pepper and cumin powder into the breadcrumbs. Take the chicken out of the marinade, letting the excess drip off, and roll in the spicy crumbs, ensuring an even coating on all sides. Dip into the egg and add a second coating of crumbs.

Place the chicken in the oiled roasting tin and cook for 20 minutes. Then lower the oven temperature to 200°C/400°F/gas mark 6, turn the chicken over and cook for another 15–25 minutes (depending on the size of the joints) or until cooked through. Serve with lemon wedges.

The flavours are clean and simple and the cooking process is easy. I like to serve these fresh from the oven, so all I do is throw them in when my friends are having their first drink and they are ready just in time.

800g chicken joints, skinned and forked all over
3 tbsp vegetable oil
¼ tsp salt
¼ tsp freshly ground black pepper
¾ tsp cumin powder
4 slices of white bread, crumbed
1 large egg, beaten
1 lemon, cut into wedges, to serve

Marinade
10g fresh ginger, peeled and roughly chopped
25g garlic (approximately 9 large cloves), peeled
2–4 green chillies, seeds and membranes removed, if wanted
1 tsp salt, or to taste
1 tsp garam masala
1 tbsp lemon juice
2 tbsp vegetable oil

my chicken
KORMA

SERVES 4

Mix the marinade ingredients together in a non-metallic bowl, add the chicken, stir and marinate for at least 30 minutes or for as long as possible. Cover and put in the fridge, if you have the time to leave it longer. Bring back to room temperature before cooking.

Heat the oil in a large non-stick pan and add the whole spices, give the pan a good stir and add the onion, green chillies and salt. Fry for about 6 minutes until the onions are golden. Add the chicken along with the marinade and the water. Turn the heat up and bring to the boil, then simmer, covered, over a lowish heat for about 25–35 minutes, depending on the size of the joints, until the chicken is tender, stirring every now and then. Add a splash of water if the pan is getting dry at any stage. Stir in the coconut and almonds, and cook, uncovered, for another 3 minutes until the gravy is creamy.

Add the garam masala, sugar and fresh coriander, taste and adjust seasoning. Serve with rice or roti (see page 127).

In this recipe I have tried to restrain my use of the heavier dairy products, but if you wish you can replace some of the yoghurt in the marinade with cream. I think this curry is delicious and it's really quick and easy to make.

700g bone-in small chicken joints, skinned and cleaned
2 tbsp vegetable oil or ghee
10 black peppercorns
10 green cardamom pods
1 black cardamom pod
10 cloves
1 shard of cinnamon
1 piece of mace
1–2 green chillies, left whole
salt and freshly ground black pepper, to taste
1 medium onion, peeled and chopped
200ml water
70g creamed coconut
3 tbsp ground almonds
¾ tsp garam masala
good pinch of sugar
handful of fresh coriander leaves and stalks, chopped

Marinade
200ml plain yoghurt
1 heaped tbsp garlic paste
1 heaped tbsp ginger paste
2 tsp coriander powder

green coriander
CHICKEN

Blend together the ingredients for the paste, reserving 10g of coriander.

Heat the oil in a non-stick saucepan and fry the onion until soft and beginning to brown. Add the paste and cook for 10 minutes, stirring often over a moderate to high heat, adding a splash of water if necessary. Then stir in the chicken, water, salt and butter and bring to a boil. Cover and cook over a low heat until the chicken is cooked, around 25–35 minutes.

Uncover and cook off all the extra water in the pan over a high heat, stirring often. Then adjust the seasoning and stir in the lemon juice. Chop the reserved coriander and stir in. Serve with any flat bread or rice.

For me, the colour green, when linked to food, means freshness and herby undernotes. This is a delicious dish where the coriander is used for taste, rather than for fragrance and texture.

1 tbsp vegetable oil
½ medium onion, peeled and chopped
1kg chicken, skinned and cut into small joints
200ml water
salt, to taste
1 tbsp butter
1 tbsp lemon juice, or to taste

Paste
120g fresh coriander stalks
1 medium onion, peeled and quartered
1–2 green chillies, halved
20g garlic (approximately 7 large cloves), peeled
12g fresh ginger, peeled
12 black peppercorns
1 tsp coriander seeds
1 tsp cumin seeds
1 tbsp white poppy seeds
2 cloves
1 shard of cinnamon
6 green cardamom pods

classic northern
CHICKEN CURRY

SERVES 6–8

Heat the oil in a large non-stick saucepan. Add the whole spices and fry for about 20 seconds until aromatic. Add the onion and cook over a moderate heat for about 10 minutes until a rich golden brown, stirring often.

Stir in the ginger and garlic and cook for a further 40 seconds before adding the salt and powdered spices, stir for a further 10 seconds. Pour in the tomatoes and cook over a moderate heat for about 10 minutes until the liquid in the pan has dried off and the oil leaves the sides of the dry masala.

Add the chicken and brown over moderate to high heat for 3–4 minutes. Add enough water to almost cover the chicken, bring to a boil and then cook over a slow to moderate heat until the chicken is cooked through. The slower it cooks, the better it tastes. This takes about 15–20 minutes for small joints and up to 25–30 minutes for larger ones.

Stir in the garam masala and coriander leaves just before serving.

This recipe is from Punjab and for an Indian this would be enough of a description. We know to expect the robust flavours of onions, tomatoes, ginger, garlic and garam masala.

4 tbsp vegetable oil
7 cloves
3 shards of cinnamon
7 green cardamom pods
2 small-medium onions, peeled and finely chopped
3 tbsp finely chopped fresh ginger
25g garlic (approximately 9 large cloves), peeled and finely chopped
salt, to taste
1 tsp turmeric
1 tsp red chilli powder
2 scant tbsp coriander powder
4 medium cooking tomatoes, puréed
900g small chicken or 2 poussins, skinned and jointed
700ml water, or more if needed
1 tsp garam masala
handful of fresh coriander leaves

chicken
BURGERS

MAKES 4

Mix together all the ingredients for the burgers, leaving out the onion rings. Allow the mixture to rest for 10 minutes in the fridge. Preheat the oven to 200°C/400°F/gas mark 6.

Mould the mince into four burgers and place on an oiled baking sheet. Place in the oven and cook for 10 minutes, turning halfway through the cooking time.

Meanwhile, mix the mayonnaise with the coriander and mint leaves, lemon, salt and pepper. Warm the burger buns in the oven for the final 2 minutes of cooking time.

Place a small handful of the lettuce on the bottom of each bun with the sliced tomato and onion rings and a good dollop of the herbed mayonnaise. Top with the hot burgers and finish off with the top half of the bun.

You can leave out the chillies when making them for children and stir them in before cooking up a batch for yourselves. Also, some may still want the taste of ketchup instead of the chutney-flavoured mayo.

Burgers
400g chicken mince
6g ginger, peeled and finely chopped
10g garlic (approximately 3 large cloves), peeled and finely chopped
1 small onion, peeled, half finely chopped (for the burgers) and half sliced into rings (for serving)
large handful of fresh coriander leaves and stalks, finely chopped
1 heaped tsp salt
¾ tsp garam masala
1½ slices of medium-cut bread, crumbed
1 egg
1 tsp cumin powder
1 tsp lemon juice
1–2 green chillies (optional), chopped and seeded
1 tbsp vegetable oil, plus extra for oiling the pan

To serve
7 tbsp light mayonnaise
2 tbsp chopped fresh coriander leaves
2 tsp chopped fresh mint leaves
1–2 tsp lemon juice, or to taste
salt, to taste
¼–½ tsp black pepper, or to taste
4 burger buns, halved
lettuce leaves, shredded
1 beef tomato, sliced

peppercorn chicken
WITH SHREDDED GINGER

Make a paste with the garlic, ginger, garam masala and chicken stock. Tip into a non-metallic bowl, add the chicken, stir to coat well and marinate in the fridge for at least 1 hour or for as long as possible. Return to room temperature before cooking.

Heat the oil in a non-stick saucepan. Add the onion and sauté for about 8 minutes or until brown. Add the green chillies, ginger, coriander powder and salt and cook for 30–40 seconds.

Add the chicken with the marinade and sear on all sides, about 3–4 minutes. Add the water and black pepper and bring to a boil. Then lower the heat, cover and simmer for 20–30 minutes until the chicken is tender. Stir the pan occasionally, adding splashes of hot water if necessary.

Increase the heat and stir the chicken for at least 3–4 minutes to reduce the gravy to just a few tablespoons. Stir in the garam masala, lemon juice and coriander just before serving.

This dish is one of our family basics and whenever certain friends came over for dinner they hoped, nay, almost asked in advance, for this dish. I soon anticipated the question and made it almost to order.

1kg chicken joints, skinned with all visible fat removed
3 tbsp vegetable oil
1 small onion, peeled and finely chopped
1–2 green chillies, to taste
15g fresh ginger, peeled and sliced into thin shreds
1 tbsp coriander powder
salt, to taste
200ml water
1 tbsp black peppercorns, coarsely ground, or to taste
½ tsp garam masala
2 tsp lemon juice
2 handfuls of chopped fresh coriander leaves and stalks

Marinade
30g garlic (approximately 10 large cloves), peeled
10g fresh ginger, peeled
1 tsp garam masala
1 chicken stock cube, dissolved in 3 tbsp hot water

himalayan lamb
& YOGHURT CURRY

Place the bay leaves, ginger, black cardamom pods, cinnamon, half the cloves, half the green cardamom pods, mace, salt, peppercorns and 3 teaspoons of the ground fennel seeds in a non-stick saucepan along with the meat and the water. Bring to a boil, then cover and cook on a low heat for about 35 minutes until the meat is tender.

Stir in the yoghurt and bring to a gentle simmer, then cook on a low heat for another 10 minutes. Add a splash of boiled water from the kettle if necessary.

Meanwhile, heat the oil or ghee in a small pan and add the remaining cloves and cardamom pods, cook for 20 seconds and stir into the meat with the garam masala and remaining ground fennel seeds. Check the seasoning and serve with plain boiled rice.

The dish has a pale, thin, flavourful and aromatic gravy that is delicious with rice or Indian bread. If the gravy has reduced too much, add a little boiled water from the kettle.

- 2 bay leaves
- ¾ tsp ground ginger
- 2 black cardamom pods
- 2 shards of cinnamon
- 8 small cloves
- 10 green cardamom pods
- 1 piece of mace
- ¾ tsp salt
- 12 black peppercorns, lightly pounded
- 4 good tsp ground fennel seeds
- 600g cubes of lamb, with the bone in
- 250ml water
- 300ml plain yoghurt
- 2 tbsp oil or ghee
- ¾ tsp garam masala
- salt, to taste

This curry's flavour is provided entirely by the spices, yoghurt and meat, and for this reason, all should be good quality and the meat should be cooked on the bone as this provides much of the lamb's flavour.

curried lamb
MEATBALLS

SERVES 4

Mix all the ingredients for the meatballs, adding 3 tablespoons of the chopped onion.

Heat the oil in a deep non-stick saucepan. Add the bay leaves, cinnamon shard and remaining chopped onion and fry until the onion is golden brown.

Meanwhile, purée the tomatoes, ginger and garlic and add to the pan. Cook over a medium heat until the oil comes to the surface, about 7–8 minutes, then add 200ml of the water and continue cooking until all the water has evaporated. Stir-fry this paste for 3 minutes, then add the powdered spices and salt. Add the remaining water, cover, bring to a boil and simmer for 5–6 minutes while you form walnut-sized meatballs from the mince.

Add the meatballs to the pan, cover and simmer for 20 minutes, shaking the pan every so often but do not stir as the meatballs can break. Add the coriander, shake the pan and serve.

This is a great dish for the whole family without the chilli (add a little paprika for colour). Serve with basmati rice or with buttery noodles.

1 medium-large onion, peeled and finely chopped
3 tbsp vegetable oil
2 bay leaves
1 small shard of cinnamon
2½ medium cooking tomatoes
8g fresh ginger, peeled
10g garlic (approximately 3 large cloves), peeled
800ml water
½ tsp turmeric
¼–¾ tsp red chilli powder, or to taste
2 tsp coriander powder
1 tsp garam masala
salt, to taste
good handful of fresh coriander stalks and leaves, chopped

Meatballs
400g lamb mince
2 tbsp finely chopped fresh coriander leaves and stalks
¾ tsp garam masala
1 tsp finely chopped ginger
10g garlic (approximately 3 cloves), peeled and finely chopped
1 large egg
½ tsp salt

herby
LAMB CHOPS

SERVES 4

Heat the oil in a non-stick saucepan and fry the onion until past golden. Add chillies and the lamb chops and brown on both sides, stirring often. Then add the garlic, ginger and garam masala and stir for 30 seconds.

Add the salt and water, bring to a boil, then cover and cook over a low-moderate heat for 15 minutes – the lamb should be cooked by now. Dry off all the excess water in the pan over a high heat, stirring often.

Purée 100g of the coriander with the mint and yoghurt. Stir into the lamb and cook for a further 15 minutes over a moderate heat until there is little gravy remaining. Adjust the seasoning, chop and add the remaining coriander and drizzle with a little lemon juice, if necessary. Serve with flat bread.

3 tbsp vegetable oil
1 medium onion, peeled and sliced
2–4 green chillies, left whole
600g lamb chops, trimmed of any excess fat
10g garlic (approximately 3 large cloves), peeled and chopped
2 tsp chopped fresh ginger
1 tsp garam masala
salt, to taste
200ml water
110g fresh coriander stalks
4 sprigs of fresh mint, leaves only
4 tbsp plain yoghurt
lemon juice, to taste

These chops are cooked simply with some basic flavourings, then have a large helping of coriander and mint added to the gravy. These mellow with cooking so that the end result is not too herby but very aromatic and flavourful.

honey-roasted spicy
LEG OF LAMB

SERVES 5–6

Blend together all the ingredients for the marinade.

Trim the lamb of the excess fat and membranes. Make deep, regular cuts all over the flesh with a short, sharp knife. Rub in the marinade, making sure you work it into the deep cuts. Place the lamb in a plastic food bag with any remaining marinade and leave in the fridge for 24 hours if possible, or for at least 6–8 hours.

Blend together 70g of the almonds, the yoghurt and half the honey. Rub into the lamb and ideally leave in the fridge for another 2 hours, but even 30 minutes will help. Bring to room temperature before cooking.

Preheat the oven to 225°C/425°F/gas mark 7. Place the lamb on a rack with a roasting tray underneath. Cook for 15 minutes, then lower the heat to 180°C/350°F/gas mark 4. Cook for 20–25 minutes per 500g plus another 15 minutes depending on how pink you like your lamb. Baste the lamb every 20–30 minutes or so with the juices that have dripped into the roasting tray.

Scatter over the remaining almonds and drizzle over the remaining honey and roast for another 10 minutes. If you wish, check the lamb with a meat thermometer – you are looking for a temperature of 130–150°C, and the higher the temperature, the more cooked the meat.

Remove the lamb from the oven and allow it to rest for 15 minutes, covered with foil. Pour the gravy into a jug and skim off any excess fat. Carve the meat and serve the gravy on the side.

2.2kg leg of lamb
100g blanched almonds
100ml thick Greek-style yoghurt
1½ tbsp honey

Marinade
2 tbsp vegetable oil
5 tbsp lemon juice
15g fresh ginger, peeled and roughly chopped
20g garlic (approximately 6 large cloves), peeled and roughly chopped
1 tbsp cumin powder
1 tbsp coriander powder
¼ tsp red chilli powder
1 tbsp garam masala
salt, to taste
½ tsp freshly ground black pepper
2 tbsp water

easy all-in-one
LAMB CURRY

Mix the lamb with the yoghurt, turmeric, ginger and garlic pastes, cumin, coriander and mustard seed powder, poppy seed paste and salt. Leave to marinate in a non-metallic bowl for as long as possible or at least until you chop and cook the next batch of ingredients.

Heat the oil in a non-stick saucepan, add the onion and green chillies and fry until the onions are brown, around 6–7 minutes. Add the meat and its marinade and stir-fry over a low heat for 3 minutes. Cover and continue to cook over a low heat for 45–50 minutes or until done, giving the pot a gentle stir every now and then. If the pan is running dry, add a splash of water from the kettle.

Once tender, stir in the garam masala and black pepper; check and adjust seasoning. Always make sure there is enough water in the pan for a little gravy by adding extra from the kettle or cook the lamb over a high flame to dry off any excess water. Stir in the coriander and serve.

WHOLE GARAM MASALA: to add a bigger punch, add 1 black cardamom pod, 4 green cardamom pods, 1 shard of cinnamon, 3 cloves and 1 piece of mace.

This is a fantastic, full-of-flavour yet mild curry, but for a spicier version add some garam masala (see above) to the hot oil before starting. I fork the chillies before adding them to prevent them bursting in the pan.

800g lamb, cut into small pieces with the bone in
300ml plain yoghurt
¾ tsp turmeric powder
1 tbsp ginger paste
1 tbsp garlic paste
1 tsp cumin powder
2 tsp coriander powder
1 tsp ground mustard seeds (ideally grind them yourself in a spice grinder)
1 heaped tbsp white poppy seeds, made into a paste (I use a pestle and mortar and a splash of water)
salt, to taste
5 tbsp vegetable oil
1 large onion, peeled and finely chopped
1–2 green chillies, forked once
1 tsp garam masala
½ tsp freshly ground black pepper
good handful of fresh coriander stalks and leaves, chopped

lamb burgers with
HERBED YOGHURT

MAKES 6

Using a hand blender, finely chop the onion, ginger, garlic, coriander and green chillies by pulsing or chop them all by hand. Add to the mince along with the remaining ingredients.

Shape into six burgers and chill for 20 minutes or until you want to eat, taking them out of the fridge 30 minutes before you want to start cooking.

Meanwhile, mix together all the ingredients for the herbed yoghurt and season to taste.

Heat the oven or grill and cook the burgers on a well-oiled grill or baking sheet for 10 minutes, turning them halfway. I like to add the hamburger buns to the oven for 3–4 minutes before I take the burgers out.

Serve in warmed hamburger buns on a bed of lettuce, tomato and onion rings with a good spoonful of the herbed yoghurt on the top.

The succulent burgers are packed with interesting flavours and they work beautifully with the cool herbed yoghurt and the fresh crunch of the vegetables.

1 small onion, peeled
12g fresh ginger, peeled
15g garlic (approximately 4 large
    cloves), peeled
20g fresh coriander stalks and leaves
2–3 green chillies, chopped, or ½–1
    tsp red chilli powder
450g lamb mince (beef mince can
    also be used)
¾ tsp cumin powder
1½ tsp garam masala
1 rounded tsp salt, or to taste
1 large egg
2 slices of thick-cut white bread,
    crumbed, or enough to bind well
2 tbsp vegetable oil, plus extra for
    oiling

Herbed yoghurt
300ml Greek-style thick yoghurt
30g fresh coriander leaves,
15g fresh mint leaves or 1 tbsp
    good-quality dried mint
1–2 green chillies (optional)
salt, to taste
½–1 tsp freshly ground black pepper

To serve
6 hamburger buns
lettuce leaves
2 plum tomatoes, sliced crosswise
1 onion, peeled and sliced crosswise
    into large rings

dry coconut
LAMB

SERVES 6

Dry roast the coconut in a non-stick pan until a little past golden. Reserve.

Heat the oil in a non-stick saucepan, add the onions and cook over a moderate heat until they are well browned. Add the ginger and garlic pastes and the turmeric and chilli powder; cook for about 30 seconds, adding a splash of water from the kettle if the pan is too dry. Add the tomatoes and salt and cook until they have broken down and the oil leaves the sides of the masala, around 10–15 minutes.

Add the lamb and brown over a moderate heat for a few minutes. Add the water, bring to a boil, then cover and simmer over a low heat for 40–50 minutes until the lamb is cooked through. If the pan is running dry at any time, add a splash of water from the kettle. Once cooked, uncover and dry off any excess water over a high heat, stirring often.

When there is only a little liquid left, stir in the garam masala. Check and adjust the seasoning, then stir in the roasted coconut and serve.

100g desiccated coconut
3 tbsp vegetable oil
2 small onions, peeled and finely sliced
1 tbsp ginger paste
1 tbsp garlic paste
½ tsp turmeric
½ tsp red chilli powder
4 medium cooking tomatoes, chopped
salt, to taste
900g lamb, cut into 2.5cm pieces with the bone in
400ml water
1 tsp garam masala

Leaving the meat on the bone adds flavour – you can ask your butcher to prepare the meat for you.

lamb with
SQUAT GREEN CHILLIES

Blend the ingredients for the marinade until smooth and pour into a non-metallic bowl. Add the lamb, stir and leave to marinate for as long as possible.

Heat 2 tablespoons of the oil, add the cumin and nigella seeds and fry for about 30 seconds until the cumin browns. Pour in the meat and its marinade and stir-fry over a moderate heat until the masala is cooked, around 12–14 minutes. Taste – it should have no harsh elements. Add the water and bring to a boil, then lower the heat, cover and cook until the lamb is tender, around 35–40 minutes. Keep checking the pot for water and give it a good stir from time to time.

Halfway through cooking the lamb, heat the remaining oil in a small pan and gently fry the chillies for 2 minutes, stirring often. Pour into the cooking meat.

Once the lamb is cooked, uncover and stir in the tamarind paste. Taste and adjust the seasoning, add water from the kettle or dry off any excess – you are looking for a curry that is neither watery nor dry but creamy. Stir in the coriander and serve with naan or rice.

The fat chillies are full of that inimitable green chilli flavour but without the killer bite of the smaller ones.

800g lamb, cut into small cubes with the bone in
3 tbsp vegetable oil
1 tsp cumin seeds
½ tsp nigella seeds
500ml water
5–8 fat, short green chillies, slit and seeds removed
2–3 tsp tamarind paste
2 handfuls of fresh coriander leaves and stalks, chopped

Marinade
1 tsp turmeric
1 tsp fennel seed powder
1 tsp garam masala
1 tbsp white poppy seeds
salt, to taste
10g garlic (about 3 large cloves), peeled
15g fresh ginger, peeled and roughly chopped
1 large onion, peeled and chopped
2 medium cooking tomatoes

green
FISH CURRY

SERVES 4–6

Heat the oil in a non-stick pan, add the whole spices and cook for 20 seconds. Add the chopped onion and fry for about 4–5 minutes until soft.

Meanwhile, blend together the remaining uncut onion, the ginger, garlic, coriander powder and 100ml of the coconut milk to a smooth purée. Add to the pan with the whole green chillies and salt and cook, covered, for 12–15 minutes, giving the pot an occasional stir.

Stir in the remaining coconut milk and spices, water, curry leaves and fish. Leave to cook undisturbed for about 3–5 minutes, depending on the thickness of the fish.

Gently stir in the lemon juice and the coriander. Check the seasoning and serve with rice.

You can use almost any firm-fleshed fish – I love it with salmon and the pale peach and green colours are a picture on a plate.

4 tbsp vegetable oil
½ tsp brown mustard seeds
4 cloves
6 green cardamom pods
1 large shard of cinnamon
1 small onion, peeled, half finely chopped and half uncut
10g fresh ginger, peeled and quartered
5g garlic (approximately 2 large cloves), peeled
1 tsp coriander powder
300ml coconut milk
2–4 green chillies, left whole
salt, to taste
½–1 tsp black pepper
¾ tsp garam masala
100ml water
10 curry leaves
500g salmon or firm white fish fillets, cut crosswise into large pieces
2–3 tsp lemon juice
50g fresh coriander leaves and stalks, chopped

spiced crab cakes with
TAMARIND MAYONNAISE

Preheat the oven to 170°C/350°F/gas mark 4.

Heat 1½ tablespoons of the oil in a pan and fry the onion for about 4 minutes until soft. Add the ginger and garlic and cook for another 40 seconds. Stir in the coriander powder, red chilli powder, salt and garam masala and cook for another 20 seconds, then take off the heat. Add the lemon juice, fresh coriander, crab, egg and mayonnaise. Stir well and add the breadcrumbs. Divide into eight portions and form into round cakes.

Heat 1 tablespoon of oil in a pan and cook the crab cakes in batches, depending how big your pan is, over a low-moderate heat, for about 2 minutes on each side until golden. Place them on a baking tray in the oven to keep warm while you cook the rest. Add the remaining oil when cooking the second batch of cakes.

To make the tamarind mayonnaise, simply whisk all the ingredients together, taste and adjust seasoning. Serve the crab cakes with a spoon of the mayo with salad leaves on the side.

Add tamarind to taste as different brands have varying levels of tartness, or use lemon juice and rind which do the same job.

3½–4½ tbsp vegetable oil
1 small onion, peeled and finely chopped
10g fresh ginger, peeled and finely chopped
5g garlic (approximately 2 small cloves), peeled and finely chopped
2 tsp coriander powder
¼–½ tsp red chilli powder
salt, to taste
1 tsp garam masala
2 tbsp lemon juice
25g fresh coriander leaves and stalks, chopped
400g prepared crab meat
1 large egg
2½ tbsp mayonnaise
9–10 pieces of thick bread, crumbed
lightly-dressed soft salad leaves, to serve

Tamarind mayonnaise
80g mayonnaise
50ml milk
salt, to taste
¼ tsp freshly ground black pepper
1 scant tbsp tamarind paste, or to taste
handful of fresh coriander leaves and stalks, chopped

coconut & chilli
PAN-FRIED HALIBUT

SERVES 2

Pound or blend together the marinade ingredients to make a fine purée. Over-season the mixture slightly as it will be absorbed by the fish. Place the fish in the marinade in a non-metallic bowl and leave for at least 30 minutes.

Mix together the coconut and the flour. Maintaining a generous coating of the purée, coat both sides of the fish steaks well in the dry mixture.

Heat the oil in a large non-stick saucepan and, when hot, add the fish. Cook on a low heat without moving the fish for 4 minutes, then turn over and cook on the other side for a further 3–4 minutes or until done. Squeeze some lemon juice over the fish and serve hot with a salad.

This delicious recipe works beautifully with any firm white-fleshed fish, so find out what is fresh at your local fishmonger. I like to serve this fish with Chopped Salad with Coconut and Peanuts (see page 103).

2 halibut steaks or other firm
   white fish
2 heaped tbsp desiccated coconut
2 heaped tbsp flour
1½ tbsp vegetable oil
½ lemon, to serve

Marinade
¾–1 large fat red chilli, deseeded
   and roughly chopped
10g fresh ginger, peeled and
   roughly chopped
10g garlic (approximately 3 large
   cloves), peeled and roughly
   chopped
2 tsp white wine vinegar
2 tsp coriander powder
8 fenugreek seeds
salt, to taste
¼ tsp freshly ground black pepper
1 tsp vegetable oil

bengali-style
BAKED FISH

Preheat the oven to 190°C/375°F/gas mark 5.

Make a paste of the poppy seeds, mustard seeds, yoghurt, ginger and chilli. I use a pestle and mortar but you can also use a blender. Stir in the salt, pepper, coriander powder and fresh coriander. Taste and adjust the seasoning.

Place the fish in a well-oiled roasting tin. Coat the top of the fish with a good layer of the paste and dot with the butter. Cook for 7–10 minutes, or until tender (it depends on the type of fish and the thickness). Drizzle with lemon juice and serve.

I love this dish – it takes just minutes to prepare, the same to cook and tastes wonderful. Serve with fresh vegetables or with the Warm Corn, Coconut and Watercress (see page 99).

1 tbsp white poppy seeds
1 tsp mustard seeds
2 heaped tbsp plain yoghurt
6g fresh ginger, peeled and
   chopped
½–1 green chilli, chopped
salt, to taste
good pinch of black pepper
1 tsp coriander powder
15g fresh coriander stalks and
   leaves, chopped (a good
   handful)
2 pieces of white-fleshed fillets,
   such as haddock or sole
vegetable oil
10g butter
lemon juice, to taste

prawn curry
WITH RICE DUMPLINGS

For the dumplings, mix all the ingredients in a bowl until you have a soft, pliable dough. Divide and roll into 12 balls or into any shape you like – I like to squeeze them in my palm to make some indentations which catch pools of curry in them. Steam for 12 minutes and set aside.

Meanwhile, start the curry. Using a pestle and mortar or spice grinder, grind the whole spices to a fine powder.

Heat the oil in a non-stick pan and fry the onion until light brown. Add the garlic paste and sauté until they smell cooked, around 1–2 minutes. Add all the ground spices and salt and cook for another minute. Add 200ml water and cook over a moderate flame until completely reduced.

Add the coconut cream, remaining water and tamarind and bring to a boil. Cook over a moderate heat for 10 minutes. Taste and adjust the tamarind paste. Add the prawns and simmer over a low heat for 3–4 minutes. Add the dumplings and simmer for another minute, or until the prawns are cooked and the dumplings warmed through.

Dumplings
100g rice flour
½ tsp salt
80–90ml warm water
20g creamed coconut, grated

Curry
1 tsp cumin seeds
2 tsp coriander seeds
9 black peppercorns
¾ tsp mustard seeds
¾ tsp turmeric powder
good pinch of carom seeds
1–2 tsp red chilli powder or
    to taste
1 tbsp garlic paste
1 large onion, peeled and finely
    chopped
80g creamed coconut, broken up
600ml water
4 tbsp vegetable or coconut oil
1½–2 tsp tamarind paste
salt, to taste
400g prawns, shelled but with the
    tail left intact and cleaned

prawn
BALCHAO

Make a paste of the ginger, garlic, red chillies and all the spices, using a little water until you achieve a fine paste.

Heat the oil in a large non-stick saucepan and fry the onion until golden brown. Add the tomatoes and green chilli and fry for about 10–12 minutes over a moderate to high heat until the mixture becomes a deep burgundy colour. Add a splash of water whenever the pan runs dry.

Add the spice paste and fry for about 5 minutes until the oil leaves the masala. Add the vinegar, sugar and a good amount of salt. Cook for another minute and taste for the balance of flavours. Adjust as you like.

Add the prawns and cook for about 2 minutes until done. To keep as a pickle, store in sterilised jars in the fridge.

A little goes a long way as it is spicy but very moreish and is an accompaniment rather than a main dish. If you want to use it as a pickle and keep it for a while, fry the prawns before adding them to the masala paste so there is no more moisture left in them.

8g fresh ginger, peeled
15g garlic (approximately 4 large cloves), peeled
1–5 dried, mild red chillies (depending on your tolerance and the quality of chillies)
2 cloves
6 peppercorns
1 tsp cumin seeds
½ tbsp brown mustard seeds
½ tsp turmeric
2½ tbsp vegetable oil
1 small onion, peeled and finely chopped
2 medium tomatoes, finely chopped
1 green chilli, left whole
3–4 tbsp malt or red wine vinegar, or to taste
1 tsp sugar
salt, to taste
350g small raw prawns, shelled and cleaned

mussels with
DRY COCONUT

Heat the oil in a medium non-stick pan and fry the onion until golden brown. Add the chillies, garlic and ginger pastes and salt and stir well for 20 seconds. Add the tomatoes and cook for about 8 minutes, or until they have softened and start to break down.

Meanwhile, cook the mussels in a large pot of boiling water until they have opened, around 3 minutes. Remove them with a slotted spoon and set aside. Reserve the water. Discard any mussels that have not opened.

Add the turmeric, garam masala and coconut to the onion mixture and mix well. Then stir in the cooked mussels – some on and some off their shell works best. Add a good splash of the cooking water and stir through. Stir in the coriander and serve with chapatti, naan or even chunks of bread.

I serve this dish with some of the mussels in their shells and others taken out and stirred into the curry, making an appetising and dramatic plate.

3 tbsp vegetable oil

1 small onion, peeled and finely chopped

2–4 green chillies, left whole

15g garlic (approximately 4 large cloves), peeled and made into a paste

10g fresh ginger, peeled and made into a paste

salt, to taste

3 tomatoes, chopped into large dice

1kg mussels, scrubbed under water and de-bearded; discard any that are already open

½ tsp turmeric powder

1 tbsp garam masala

70g desiccated coconut

handful of fresh coriander leaves and stalks, chopped

vegetables

southern indian
MIXED VEGETABLE DISH

SERVES 6

Soak the coconut in water to cover while you prepare the vegetables.

Heat the oil in a large non-stick pan. Add the cumin, onion and chillies and sauté for about 4–5 minutes until the onions are soft and colouring. Add the turmeric, salt, potatoes and carrots and cook for 14 minutes, covered, over a low heat. Stir frequently to make sure the vegetables don't catch on the base of the pan, adding a sprinkle of water if necessary. Add the cucumber and beans and continue cooking in the same manner until the vegetables are all tender, a further 6–7 minutes or so.

Meanwhile, blend together the shallots, ginger and coconut, along with its soaking water, to make a fine paste. Add to the pan with the peas and cook, stirring often, for 5 minutes. Tear the curry leaves to release their aroma and add to the pan, give it a good stir and add the yoghurt. Turn off the heat and mix well, pouring over the coconut oil, if using.

The dish is often served at feasts, but I have reduced the amount of oil and coconut used and happily eat it for lunch with some rice or as part of a meal.

50g desiccated coconut
2½ tbsp vegetable oil
1 tsp cumin seeds
½ medium onion, peeled and sliced
1–2 green chillies, slit lengthwise but left whole
¼ tsp turmeric
salt, to taste
2 medium potatoes, peeled and cut into quarters lengthwise and then sliced crosswise on the diagonal
2 medium carrots, peeled and cut into fat batons
15cm piece of cucumber, halved lengthwise, seeds scooped out and cut crosswise into 1cm pieces
100g green beans, topped and tailed and sliced lengthwise on the diagonal into three
50g shallots, peeled and halved
10g fresh ginger, peeled and roughly chopped
2 handfuls of frozen peas
12 curry leaves
5 level tbsp plain yoghurt (fresh, not sour)
1 tbsp coconut oil (optional)

stir-fried spring ONIONS

Heat the oil in a small non-stick saucepan. Add the cumin seeds and fry until lightly coloured and fragrant. Add the rest of the spices, stir-fry for just 5–10 seconds, then add the spring onions. Turn the heat up and stir-fry for 1 minute – they should still remain crunchy. Taste and adjust the seasoning and serve straightaway.

1 tbsp vegetable oil
½ tsp cumin seeds
½ tsp turmeric powder
1 tsp coriander powder
pinch of red chilli powder
bunch of spring onions, preferably
   thin ones, washed and sliced
   into small rounds, around
5–7.5mm long
salt, to taste

warm corn, coconut & WATERCRESS

SERVES 3–4

Heat the butter and oil in a small, non-stick saucepan and add the mustard seeds. Cook for a few seconds, covering the pan once they start to pop. Add the curry leaves, ginger and chillies and give the pan a good stir. Add the corn and milk; cook over a moderate heat for 12-15 minutes until there is little moisture left in the pan.

To serve, season and stir in the coconut, watercress and lemon juice to taste.

1 tbsp butter
1 tsp vegetable oil
1 tsp mustard seeds
12 curry leaves
1 tsp chopped ginger
1-2 small red dry chillies (optional)
350g frozen or canned sweetcorn.
   drained and washed
250ml milk
satl, to taste
2 tbsp flaked coconut (or dessicated
   if you don't have flaked)
handful of watercress, washed
1 tsp lemon juice, or to taste

lentils &
BEANS

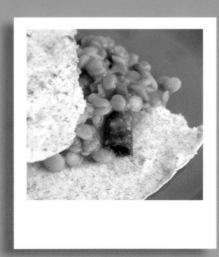

buttery black
LENTILS

SERVES 4–6

Drain the lentils, discarding their soaking water, and put in a large saucepan with the fresh water. Bring to a boil and then simmer, covered, for about 1 hour or until tender.

Meanwhile, make a paste of the garlic and half the ginger. Finely slice the remaining ginger into long, fine shreds.

When the lentils are tender, add the tomato purée, chilli powder, green chillies, salt and the garlic-ginger paste to the pan. Stir well and cook for another 30 minutes. Keep an eye on the pan and give it an occasional stir as the lentils have a tendency to settle on the base.

Heat the butter in a pan over a low heat, add the onion and sliced ginger and cook for about 4–5 minutes until coloured. Stir into the lentils along with the single cream and garam masala. Cook for a further minute and serve garnished with fresh coriander.

The lentils would traditionally be cooked overnight over the barest flame so they cook evenly and perfectly, but they are well worth the wait.

240g whole black lentils, picked through, washed and soaked for at least 3 hours
1 litre water
10g garlic (approximately 3 large cloves), peeled
15g fresh ginger, peeled and halved lengthways
180g tomato purée
½–1 tsp red chilli powder
2 green chillies, left whole
salt, to taste
30g butter
½ onion, peeled and chopped
50ml single cream
1 tsp garam masala
handful of fresh coriander, to garnish

toasted
SPICED CHICKPEAS

Heat the oil in a non-stick saucepan. Add the cumin seeds and fry for about 30–40 seconds or until they give off their aroma and start to darken. Add the remaining spices and salt and cook for 10 seconds. Add the chickpeas and stir to coat well in the spices. Cook for 2 minutes, then add the water and the coriander leaves. Cook for a further minute and serve.

The chickpeas are full of minerals and good fibre and always go down a treat. Ideally, you would eat this dish with Indian layered bread (parathas), but it also works well with naan or even toast.

2 tbsp vegetable oil
1 tsp cumin seeds
½ tsp turmeric powder
¼–¾ tsp red chilli powder
1¼ tbsp coriander powder
1 tsp dried mango powder
¾ tsp garam masala
400g can of chickpeas,
    drained and rinsed
salt, to taste
2 tbsp boiled water
handful of fresh coriander,
    chopped

simple spinach
& LENTIL CURRY

SERVES 4

Place the lentils, water, ginger, chillies and turmeric in a pan, bring to a boil, then simmer over a moderate heat for 10 minutes. Stir in the tomatoes and cook for a further 20 minutes, then add the spinach and salt. Cook for another 10 minutes or so, until the lentils have started to break down and the curry comes together.

Meanwhile, heat the ghee, butter or oil in a small pan. Add the cumin seeds and garlic and allow the cumin seeds to redden and the garlic to start to brown. Stir in the coriander powder and garam masala, then pour the mixture into the pan of lentils. Cook for another minute and serve.

This dish is so simple to make and is typical of home fare. It is the kind of dish that a mother makes for her family, is good for all ages and, despite the chillies, not really too spicy.

150g skinned and split yellow mung lentils
900ml water
8g fresh ginger, peeled and cut into thin strips
3 green chillies, left whole (optional)
¾ tsp turmeric powder
2 small tomatoes, puréed
200g baby spinach leaves
salt, to taste
1½ tbsp ghee, butter or vegetable oil
1 tsp cumin seeds
5g garlic (approximately 2 cloves), peeled and cut into 5 large pieces
1 rounded tsp coriander powder
½ tsp garam masala

broad bean
THORAN

Heat the oil in a pan, add the seeds and fry for 30 seconds. Add the onion, ginger and green chilli and cook for about 4 minutes over a lowish heat until the onions have softened.

Add the beans, salt and a splash of water and cook for 1 minute to warm through. Stir in the coconut and torn curry leaves, turn the heat down, cover, and cook for 2 minutes. Give the pan a stir and serve.

I love broad beans as they are and generally prefer not to cook them, but they are perfect in this simple south Indian dish. I feel the need to grate fresh coconut to go with these beans to retain their inherent freshness and there is a simple, inexpensive gadget called a coconut grater (see page 11) that helps me do this in minutes.

1 tbsp coconut or vegetable oil
½ tsp brown mustard seeds
½ tsp cumin seeds
½ small onion, peeled and finely chopped
1 tsp chopped fresh ginger
1 green chilli, left whole
200g fresh or frozen broad beans, podded and thawed if using frozen
salt, to taste
40g grated fresh coconut
8 fresh curry leaves, torn in half

garlic & chilli
SPLIT PIGEON PEA CURRY

SERVES 2–3

Place the water and lentils in a saucepan and bring to a boil. Add the turmeric, cover and simmer over a low heat for about 20 minutes or until tender. Uncover and cook over a moderate heat for about 10 minutes until the lentils completely break down. If the lentils are too watery, increase the heat.

Heat the ghee or oil in a separate, small non-stick saucepan. Add the chillies and cook for a minute, then add the garlic. Cook over a moderate heat until the garlic is golden but not burned, then pour straight into the pan of lentils. Add the dried mango powder, salt and lemon juice to taste – the quantities of these depend on how tart your dried mango powder is. Serve hot. This curry solidifies as it cools, so add extra water if you are going to leave it to reheat later.

500ml water
100g split pigeon pea lentils (toovar dal), picked over and washed
½ tsp turmeric powder
1 tbsp ghee or vegetable oil
2–4 small dried red chillies, whole (I use birds eye chillies)
1 rounded tbsp chopped garlic
1 level tbsp dried mango powder, or to taste
salt, to taste
1 tbsp lemon juice, or to taste

This simple dish is the arabiatta of the lentil world – spicy, garlicky and tart – using flavours that go really well with the savoury lentils. These lentils break down into a purée and as the dish cools it tends to firm up, so make sure the curry is not too thick before you take it off the heat.

slightly sweet bengal
GRAM LENTIL CURRY

SERVES 4–6

Place the lentils, bay leaves, water and turmeric in a pan, bring to a boil and then simmer, covered for around 50–60 minutes or until soft. Add extra water, if necessary.

Stir in the coriander and garam masala, salt and sugar to taste. Cook until the lentils are completely soft and start to break up – I have an Indian wooden whisk that is ideal for this, but try anything that helps to break them up a little. You should be left with a thick lentily mass but with the actual lentils still discernible.

To serve, heat the oil or butter in a small pan (if using mustard oil, heat until smoking then cool and reheat) and fry the cardamom pods, cumin, cloves, cinnamon, mustard seeds and chillies for 30 seconds. Add the coconut and cook until it turns golden, then pour the mixture over the lentils. Stir in or leave to stir at the table.

This popular Bengali dish is simple food and subtly spiced, as is most Bengali food. The lentils are meant to be thick, sweet and savoury.

250g Bengal gram, well washed
2 bay leaves
1.2 litres water
½ tsp turmeric powder
1 heaped tsp coriander powder
1 tsp garam masala
salt, to taste
2–3 tsp sugar
2 tbsp mustard oil, unsalted butter or ghee
5 green cardamom pods
1 tsp cumin seeds
5 cloves
5cm shard of cinnamon
½ tsp brown mustard seeds
1–2 dried red chillies
3 heaped tbsp flaked or desiccated coconut, or ¼ small fresh coconut, flesh cut into small dice

bread
& RICE

basmati RICE

SERVES 4

Soak the rice in fresh, cold water for 30 minutes for long and fluffy grains.

Drain and tip into a thick-bottomed pan for even cooking. Add the water and bring to a good boil. Add the lemon juice, if using, and give it a good stir. Cover tightly, turn the heat right down and cook for 7–8 minutes. Check after 7 minutes – the grains should be cooked, but if not, cover and test again after another minute.

Turn off the heat and uncover. Allow any excess moisture to evaporate from the pan for 5 minutes, then fluff up with a fork and serve.

200g Basmati rice, cleaned in
   several washes of water until
   the water runs clear
365ml water
½ tsp lemon juice (optional)

spinach PILAFF

SERVES 3–4

Heat the oil in a large saucepan, add the whole spices and green chillies and cook for 20 seconds. Add the onion and cook for about 4 minutes until translucent. Stir in the rice, spinach and salt and stir-fry to heat through. Just before serving, add lemon juice to taste.

2 tbsp oil
1 bay leaf
2 black cardamom pods
6 black peppercorns
1 tsp cumin seeds
1–2 green chillies, forked but
   left whole
1 small onion, peeled and chopped
300g cooked Basmati rice (see
   recipe on the left for method)
200g baby spinach leaves, wilted
   in a pan and puréed
salt, to taste
2–3 tsp lemon juice, or to taste

lemon RICE

SERVES 2–3

Heat the oil in a large non-stick frying pan and add both seeds, the lentils, raw peanuts (if using) and chillies and stir-fry until the lentils are light brown. Add the ginger, turmeric powder, curry leaves and salt and cook for 40 seconds.

Add the lemon juice and cook for another minute. Add the rice and roasted peanuts (if using instead of raw peanuts). Stir-fry to heat through, being careful not to break up the grains too much. Serve hot. (See page 120 for image)

2 tbsp vegetable oil
½ tsp mustard seeds
pinch of fenugreek seeds
¾ tsp split Bengal gram
¾ tsp split black gram
3 heaped tbsp peanuts, coarsely
　chopped (raw is best)
1–2 dried red chillies, left whole
1 tsp chopped ginger
¼ tsp turmeric powder
10 curry leaves, torn in half
salt, to taste
3 tbsp lemon juice, or to taste
300g cooked Basmati rice
　(see page 121 for method)

coconut RICE

SERVES 2

Heat the oil in a large non-stick frying pan, add the mustard seeds, cumin seeds, chillies and both lentils and fry until the latter start to colour. Add the onion and ginger and cook over a moderate heat for 4 minutes or until the onion is soft.

Add salt, pepper, cashews, curry leaves, rice and soaked coconut and stir-fry over a moderate heat until the rice is hot and all the flavours combined. Check the seasoning and serve.

2 tbsp vegetable oil
½ tsp mustard seeds
½ tsp cumin seeds
2 dried red chillies, whole
1 tsp split Bengal gram
1 tsp split black gram
½ small onion, peeled and chopped
1 tsp finely chopped ginger
salt and freshly ground black
　pepper, to taste
2–3 tbsp roasted cashew nuts,
　broken up
10 curry leaves
250g cooked Basmati rice
　(see page 121 for method)
4 tbsp desiccated coconut, soaked in
　water to cover before you cook
　(it will absorb most of the water)

simple PILAFF

Heat the oil in a large non-stick saucepan. Add the cumin seeds and cook for about 30 seconds until fragrant. Add the onion and sauté for about 6 minutes until lightly caramelised. Add the garam masala and salt and cook, stirring, for another 20 seconds.

Stir in the drained rice and frozen peas, then add the water. Taste for seasoning. Bring to a boil, then cook, covered, on the lowest heat for 10 minutes. Check that the grains are tender; if not, leave to steam for another 2 minutes. Then remove the lid and allow any moisture to evaporate. Drizzle over the lemon juice and gently mix in with a fork, fluffing up the grains.

2 tbsp vegetable oil
1 tsp cumin seeds
1 small onion, peeled and thinly
   sliced
1 tsp garam masala
salt, to taste
200g Basmati or long-grain white
   rice, washed and soaked for
   30 minutes
100g frozen peas
375ml water
1–2 tbsp lemon juice, or to taste

wild mushroom PILAFF

Wash the rice well and soak in cold water while you prepare the mushrooms. If using dried mushrooms, soak in boiling water for 20 minutes, then drain. Wash the morels well and wipe the other mushrooms clean with damp kitchen paper. Cut any large mushrooms into slices.

Heat the oil in a large, wide saucepan. Add the whole spices and cook for 20 seconds, then add the onion and cashew nuts. Fry for about 4–5 minutes until the onions are soft and browning at the edges. Add the mushrooms, garlic and salt and sauté over a high heat for 4–5 minutes.

Drain the rice and add to the pan of mushrooms with the water, bring to a good boil, then cover with a lid, lower the heat and cook for 10 minutes. Taste a grain of rice to check if it's cooked; if not, leave for another minute. Take off the heat, remove the lid and allow any excess moisture to evaporate. Gently stir in the lemon juice and taste and adjust the seasoning, if necessary.

300g Basmati rice
200g good-quality wild mushrooms such as
   girolles, morels, ceps, oyster, etc
5 tbsp vegetable oil
1 small onion, peeled and chopped into 1cm dice
large handful of raw cashew nuts, whole
5g garlic (approximately 2 cloves), peeled and
   finely chopped
salt, to taste
550ml water
1 tsp lemon juice, or to taste

Whole spices
1 tsp cumin seeds
2 bay leaves
1 large shard of cinnamon
2 black cardamom pods
6 green cardamom pods
6 black peppercorns
4 cloves

simple layered
FLAT BREADS

SERVES 4–6

Mix together the flour and salt in a large bowl. Add the milk or water slowly until you have a soft, non-sticky dough (it might not require all the liquid). Knead for about 8–10 minutes, until the mixture has formed a smooth dough. Cover with a damp tea-towel and leave to rest for at least 10 minutes.

Divide the dough into 6 equal balls. Dust the balls lightly with flour. Take one and roll into a 15cm circle. Using the back of a spoon or your fingers, smear ¾ teaspoon of ghee or melted butter over the surface, sprinkle a little flour over it and a pinch of carom seeds.

Roll the bread up as you would for a tight Swiss roll, elongating the rope as you do by pulling the sides, for a long roll. Take one end of each piece of dough and coil it round on itself like rope. Press down with your fingers to flatten again. Dust with flour and roll out into a 12cm circle.

Heat a non-stick frying pan over a low heat. Place the dough onto the pan and turn the heat up a little. Once the top surface of the dough starts to dry out, turn it over. Take another ¾ teaspoon of ghee or butter and spread it over the surface. For a flaky finish, slash all over with the edge of the spoon you are using.

Once the underside has become golden, turn again and repeat with the ghee or butter and the spoon and cook until golden. Place on a plate covered with kitchen paper, cover the bread with more paper, and keep warm while you make the rest.

150g chapatti flour, (or substitute half whole-wheat and half plain flour), plus extra for sprinkling
½ tsp salt
90–110ml milk or water
3 tbsp ghee or melted butter
1 tsp carom seeds

roti

MAKES 6

Sift the flour and salt, if using, into a bowl and make a well in the centre. Slowly drizzle in most of the water and, using your hand, draw the flour into the centre, mixing all the time. You may not need all the water as flour absorbs different amounts of water. It should be just slightly sticky.

Knead for 8–10 minutes. Then place in a bowl, cover with a damp tea-towel and leave for 30 minutes in a slightly warm area or at room temperature in the summer.

Divide the dough into 6 equal portions and roll into golfball-sized rounds; cover. Flour your work surface and rolling pin. Roll each ball into thin circles 12.5–15cm in diameter. The best way of doing this is to keep rolling in one direction, turning the dough a quarter of a circle each time to get a round shape.

Heat a tava or non-stick frying pan until quite hot. Toss the roti from one hand to the other to remove any excess flour, and place in the pan. Turn the heat down to moderate and cook until small bubbles appear on the underside, about 20–30 seconds, then turn. Cook this side until the base now has small dark beige spots.

The best way to puff up a cooked roti is to place it directly over an open flame (such as on a gas hob) using tongs. It will puff immediately, but leave for 3–5 seconds until dark spots appear, then turn and leave this side for a few seconds and place on a plate. Repeat with the rest. If you have an electric hob, press down gently on the cooked roti – as you press one area, the rest should puff up. Then tackle the next area – the roti should puff up all over. Keep the bread warm by wrapping in a napkin or foil and placing in a low oven while you make the rest. You can reheat the roti, wrapped, in a medium oven.

150g chapatti flour (or half whole-wheat and half plain flour)
salt (optional)
90–110ml water

instant
NAAN

MAKES 6 MEDIUM NAAN

Preheat the oven to its highest setting (mine goes up to 275°C). Place a baking sheet on the uppermost shelf to heat through.

Mix together all the dry ingredients. Make a well in the middle and add your wet ingredients with 85–90ml of water. Bring together with your hands into a dough. Knead quickly until smooth.

Roll out into 0.75cm-thick naan breads – trying to achieve that characteristic teardrop shape – using a little more flour. Pat off any excess flour and place the breads on the hot baking sheet (you will need to do this in 2 batches). Cook for 2-4 minutes, or until there are brown spots on the upper surface. Brush with the extra melted butter, which helps to soften and brighten the surface, and serve hot.

CARAMELISED ONION TOPPING: Heat 2 tbsp vegetable oil and fry 1 sliced onion until soft. Scatter over the top of the naan before cooking.

GARLIC AND CORIANDER BUTTER NAAN: Crush 1 large garlic clove and add to a small saucepan with 2 tbsp butter. Melt the butter. Stir in 2 tbsp chopped fresh coriander and brush over the cooked naan.

SEEDED: Press 1 rounded tsp of nigella or sesame seeds, or 1 rounded tbsp pumpkin seeds, or any other seeds you like (try black onion or poppy seeds) evenly into the upper surface of the breads before baking.

300g plain flour, plus more
 to dust
¾ tsp baking powder
½ tsp bicarbonate of soda
½ tsp salt
1½ tsp sugar
4 tbsp milk
4 tbsp plain yogurt
15g butter, melted, plus more
 for brushing

raitas &
CHUTNEYS

pomegranate RAITA

Lightly press down on the pomegranate and roll with your hands on a hard surface, applying a little pressure so that you help to release the seeds on all sides. Slice in half and, working over a bowl, tap the outside of the fruit with a wooden spoon. The seeds should tumble out. There may be too many for the raita so munch away.

Mix together the yoghurt, most of the pomegranate seeds and fresh coriander. Season with salt, lots of black pepper, the cumin and red chilli powder. Garnish with a handful of pomegranate seeds and a few coriander leaves.

1 small pomegranate
400ml plain yoghurt
handful of chopped fresh
    coriander leaves and stalks
salt and freshly ground black
    pepper, to taste
½–¾ tsp roasted cumin powder
    (cumin seeds dry-roasted until
    red and ground)
good pinch of red chilli powder,
    to taste

tomato, cucumber
& ONION RAITA

SERVES 4

Mix together the vegetables, coriander and yoghurt. Season with salt, plenty of black pepper and the roasted cumin powder.

Tip into a serving bowl, sprinkle over the chilli powder and serve.

1 tomato, diced
1 small red onion, peeled and diced
12.5cm piece of cucumber, peeled
    and diced
2 tbsp fresh chopped coriander
    leaves and stalks
400ml plain yoghurt
salt and freshly ground black
    pepper, to taste
½–¾ tsp roasted cumin powder
    (cumin seeds dry-roasted until
    red and ground)
¼ tsp red chilli powder

cucumber & MINT RAITA

SERVES 4

Peel the cucumber, then coarsely grate and squeeze all the excess moisture from it.

Mix together the cucumber, mint and yoghurt. Stir in the seasoning and cumin powder. Sprinkle over the red chilli powder to serve.

Great with any meal or barbecue, or even just as a dip with naan, crudités or potato wedges.

12.5cm cucumber
3 tbsp shredded fresh mint
400ml plain yoghurt
salt and freshly ground black pepper, to taste
¾ tsp roasted cumin powder (seeds dry-roasted until red, then ground)
good pinch of red chilli powder

tangy herby CHUTNEY

SERVES 6

Blend together all the ingredients with 4 tbsp water until smooth; it might take a few minutes. Taste and adjust the seasoning. Keep in a glass jar in the fridge for a week, or freeze until ready to use.

An incredibly versatile recipe, this is the cornerstone of all North Indian snacks. We love it with samosas, bhajis, pakoras, kebabs... and most other things!

60g fresh coriander, leaves and stalks
2½ tbsp lemon juice
2 green chillies, deseeded if you prefer
12g mint leaves
20g raw or roasted unsalted peanuts
salt, to taste

quick tamarind
CHUTNEY

SERVES 6–8 SNACKS

Put all the ingredients in a small saucepan, bring to a quick boil, then turn off the heat. Cool and serve judiciously.

This chutney can also be stored in screw-top jars in the fridge. It keeps well for weeks.

Tamarind is our version of ketchup and served in even smaller quantities. Its natural partners are many of the northern tea-time snacks, such as vegetable samosas.

3 tsp thick tamarind paste
4 tbsp brown or white sugar
½ tsp cumin seeds, dry roasted until fragrant and turning brown, then ground
¼–½ tsp freshly ground black pepper
60ml water

drinks &
DESSERTS

nutty saffron
FLAVOURED YOGHURT

SERVES 4

Line a large sieve with a double layer of good-quality kitchen paper. Place over a bowl and pour in the yoghurt. Refrigerate for as long as possible, at least 5–6 hours or until all the whey has drained off.

Heat the milk and crumble the saffron strands into the hot milk. Leave to infuse for 8–10 minutes, crushing the strands in the milk with the back of a spoon or your fingers.

Sift the sugar into the yoghurt and stir in along with the saffron milk, cardamom powder and half the nuts. Taste and adjust the sugar and cardamom powder if necessary. Chill and serve garnished with the remaining nuts, pomegranate seeds and silver leaf, if using.

Yoghurt will vary in its degree of tartness, depending on freshness, so add sugar according to taste. The potency of the saffron and cardamom powder also varies, depending on freshness and quality, so use my measurements as a guide.

1 litre whole-milk yoghurt or 500ml Greek-style yoghurt
2 tsp milk
½–¾tsp saffron strands
6–8 tbsp icing sugar, or to taste (depends on the tartness of the yoghurt)
¼ tsp freshly ground green cardamom powder, or to taste
3 tbsp chopped unsalted pistachios
3 tbsp flaked or sliced almonds, lightly roasted
pomegranate seeds, to garnish
silver leaf, to garnish (optional)

steamed
YOGHURT

SERVES 4

Line a sieve with a double layer of kitchen paper and place over a large bowl. Pour in the yoghurt and allow the whey to drain off for at least 5 hours. If you wish, you can leave it, covered, in the fridge overnight, but be sure to drain away any liquid in the bowl after the first 2 hours.

Preheat the oven to 180°C/350°F/gas mark 4.

Whisk together the yoghurt, condensed milk and raisins (if using) until smooth. Divide the mixture between four small ramekins or oven-proof glasses. Cover each ramekin tightly with foil to prevent water getting in. Place them in a baking dish and pour in enough water to come a quarter of the way up the sides of the ramekins. Carefully place in the oven and cook for 30 minutes.

Cool the desserts in their pots and chill overnight. Either serve in their pots or turn out onto serving plates. Serve with the raspberries and sprinkle the nuts over the top.

500ml set natural yoghurt
95ml condensed milk
1½ tbsp raisins (optional)
20 pistachios, roughly chopped, or 2 tbsp flaked almonds, toasted
raspberries, to serve

The texture of this delicious dessert from Bengal is somewhere between a smooth panna cotta and a ricotta cheesecake. The longer you cook it, the grainier it becomes; this is not to say grainy is bad, some people prefer it one way, some the other.

strawberry LASSI

Blend the strawberries, yoghurt and sugar together until frothy. Pour into glasses and serve with the ice.

200g ripe strawberries
200ml good-quality fresh plain yoghurt
1½–3 tbsp sugar (depending on how sweet the berries are)
ice cubes, to serve

lemon LASSI

SERVES 2

Blend together the yoghurt, water, sugar, lemon juice and zest until light and frothy. Adjust the sugar and lemon to taste. Pour into tall glasses filled with ice cubes and the mint and serve.

240ml good-quality fresh plain yoghurt
200ml water
3 tbsp sugar, or to taste
2–3 tsp lemon juice, or to taste
1½ tsp finely grated lemon zest
ice cubes, to serve
2 sprigs of fresh mint

mango SMOOTHIE

SERVES 2

Standing the mango upright with the narrow end towards you, slice off both cheeks on the either side of the stone. Slice these in half lengthwise and remove the skin by peeling or slicing. Slice off the remaining sides of the stone as much as possible. Repeat with the second mango and put all the flesh and juices in a blender.

Add the milk and sugar and blend to a thick, smooth mass. Pour into glasses, each filled with ice cubes, and serve chilled.

2 Alphonso mangoes
300ml milk
2 tbsp sugar, or to taste
lots of ice cubes, to serve

kulfi

SERVES 4

Heat the milk in a wide, heavy-based pan over a low heat and bring to a boil. Then lower the heat and cook gently, stirring often. Place the ground almonds and flour in a small cup and once the milk is warm, stir in a little milk, make a thin paste and stir back into the pan with the sugar. Continue to cook gently as the milk needs to reduce by half – this takes about an hour. If a skin forms on the surface, just stir it back in.

Stir in the cardamom powder to taste. Cool completely, then decant into 4 kulfi moulds (I also know of it being set in polystyrene cups or normal freezerproof containers). If you have the time, 2 hours after it has been put into the freezer, take it out and give it a good whisk to break up any ice crystals.

I recommend keeping the ice cream in the freezer for about 5–6 hours. Take the moulds out of the freezer 20 minutes before serving. Dip them briefly in hot water to loosen, then turn out onto serving plates. Sprinkle generously with the nuts.

1 litre full-fat milk
2 tbsp ground almonds
1 tbsp rice flour
5–6 tbsp sugar, or to taste
⅓–½ tsp green cardamom powder, or to taste
2 tbsp chopped pistachios
2 tbsp flaked almonds

I have enriched my basic recipe by adding some ground almonds and rice flour, but you can make a simpler version by doubling the quantity of milk and leaving out the almonds and flour.

coconut &
JAGGERY PANCAKES

MAKES 12 SMALL PANCAKES OR 8 LARGER ONES

Sift the flour into a large bowl and add the salt and sugar. Make a well in the middle and crack in the egg, then pour in the melted butter. Using a whisk, slowly bring the sides of the flour into the well and mix until you have a smooth paste. Whisk in the milk and leave to rest for 30 minutes.

Meanwhile, mix together the ingredients for the filling.

Heat the pan until hot. Add a little butter and, when melted, pour in a ladleful or half a ladleful of batter, depending on the size of your pan. You want a thin covering. Turn the heat to medium and after 30 seconds or so, using a flat metal spatula, flip the pancake over. Cook the other side for another 15–20 seconds or until the base has a few brown spots.

Continue cooking the pancakes this way but without adding any more butter to the pan. Stack the pancakes on a plate, separating them with greaseproof paper.

When you are ready to eat, place 1–1½ heaped tablespoons of filling on one half of the pancake and fold. You can heat the filling in the pan if you wish, which will melt the jaggery, and if you heat the pancakes in the oven at the same time, this dessert will be great served with a scoop of vanilla ice cream.

Pancakes
50g plain flour
pinch of salt
1 tbsp sugar
1 egg
150ml milk
25g unsalted butter, melted,
  plus extra for frying

Filling
80g jaggery (choose the darkest
  one you can find)
140g fresh coconut, grated
80g roasted salted cashew nuts,
  broken up

sandesh
SWEETS

Bring the milk to a boil in a pan set over a low heat. Once the milk starts to rise in the pan, stir in the yoghurt. The milk will curdle, leaving curd-like cheese floating in murky water. If it does not split, add some more yoghurt and leave for 20 seconds over the heat.

Line a sieve with muslin and place over a large bowl or saucepan. Strain the cheese into the lined sieve and discard the water. Run fresh tap water over the cheese to remove any sourness from the yoghurt. Twist the muslin around the cheese to make a tight ball and place it under a weight (I fill the pan with water and place it on top). Leave to drain for 20 minutes.

Place the cheese in a blender with the sugar and pulse three times to make a slightly grainy paste. Spoon the mixture into a cold non-stick frying pan and place over a low-moderate heat, stirring continuously for about 3–5 minutes. The mixture should leave the base of the pan and have the texture of soft dough. It will dry more as it cools. If in doubt, take a small bit and roll it into a small ball. It shouldn't crack and should hold its shape without being hard.

Now the basic mixture is ready. Add the saffron and the cardamom powder and roll into small walnut-sized balls. Garnish with silver leaf, chopped pistachios, flaked almonds, saffron strands, flaked coconut or rose petals, depending on the flavouring. Chill until ready to eat.

1 litre full-fat milk
100–150ml yoghurt (depends how sour the yoghurt is), beaten
45g caster sugar
good pinch of saffron, powdered in a pestle and mortar with ¼ tsp sugar
½ tsp green cardamom powder (seeds taken out of the pods and ground)

Other flavouring ideas
1 tbsp rose water, or to taste
¾ tsp vanilla essence, or to taste
40g pistachio nuts, shelled and pounded to a rough purée (add an extra tbsp sugar to the cheese and add 1 tbsp milk)
good-quality chocolate powder, to taste
3 tbsp desiccated coconut, or to taste

To garnish
silver leaf, chopped pistachios, flaked almonds, saffron strands, flaked coconut or rose petals

DRINKS & DESSERTS **147**

orange-scented
RICE CREAMS

Mix the rice flour and ground almonds in 150ml of the milk to make a smooth paste. Heat the remaining milk in a pan on a medium heat, stirring constantly. As you bring it up to a simmer, stir in the rice-flour mixture.

Cook, stirring, over a medium heat for 10 minutes. Add the sugar, cardamom and orange rind and continue cooking for about 3–4 minutes until it reaches a semi-thick custard consistency. Pour into your serving dish of choice and chill. Garnish with the nuts and slices of orange before serving.

I set the creams in individual bowls or sometimes cocktail glasses for a little glamour, but you can use one large bowl and serve straight from there.

4½ tbsp rice flour
2 tbsp ground almonds
1 litre full-fat milk
4 tbsp sugar
½–¾ tsp green cardamom powder
1 heaped tsp grated orange rind, or to taste
10 pistachios, blanched, peeled and sliced
10 almonds, blanched, skinned and sliced, or flaked almonds
slices of blood orange, to garnish

charantais melon
RASAYANA

Place the melon dice in a deep bowl. Using your fingers, crush them slightly so that they are no longer regular in shape and start to leak out their wonderful juice, but do not let them become mushy. Add the coconut milk and sugar and mix well. The colour should be a beautiful pale peach; you may want to give the melon another crush to assimilate the two. Stir in the pomegranate and chill until ready to serve.

Place a tablespoon of crushed ice in the bottom of the serving bowls and top with the rasayana. Sprinkle over the flaked almonds and serve cold.

The Charantais melon is juicy and sweet and perfect in this refreshing south Indian-inspired dessert. The melon leaks into the creamy coconut and is lifted by the pomegranate seeds.

225g Charantais melon flesh (weighed without the skin), cut into small dice
225ml fresh or canned coconut milk
2 tbsp sugar, or to taste (depending on sweetness of melon)
seeds from ½ a pomegranate
2 handfuls of crushed ice
handful of flaked almonds, lightly roasted in the oven until just changing colour

jaggery-caramelised
WALNUTS

SERVES 3 TO MUNCH ON OR 5 AS A GARNISH

Place the jaggery in a saucepan and stir over a low-moderate heat to melt. Stir frequently to help it melt faster. When smooth, stir in the walnut halves. Stir to coat properly and cook for 1–2 minutes or until the jaggery has darkened in colour.

Place the walnuts individually on a sheet of baking paper or turn out onto an oiled plate. You have to work quickly as the jaggery will start to harden. If so, heat the pan a little to melt it again.

Store in an airtight container when cool.

100g jaggery, chopped or
   pounded into smallish pieces
80g walnut halves

The best jaggery is quite dark and hard and needs to be chopped and pestle-and-mortared. It can be found in Indian shops, and although supermarkets have started to stock it, theirs is a softer, more watery version of the real thing. Either will work, but the darker jaggery has a more molasses-like flavour.

the best MASALA TEA

Heat the water, milk, spices and ginger in a pan. Once it comes to a boil, reduce the heat and cook over a low-moderate heat for 20 minutes or until the pan looks like it is one large mugs worth. Be careful as the milk easily boils over. If this is about to happen, reduce the heat and take the pan off the heat for a few seconds.

Once reduced, add the tea bag and let it brew for 1 minute, or more if you like strong tea. Strain into your cup and add sugar or salt, to taste.

350ml water
100ml milk
4 black peppercorns
10 green cardamom pods
good pinch of green fennel seeds
small shard of cinnamon
8g fresh ginger, peeled and roughly
   sliced
1 tea bag (I use a common black
   tea blend)
sugar, to taste
slightest pinch of salt (optional)

fennel DROP-BISCUITS

Mix together the flour, sugar, powdered and whole milk, spices, salt, almonds and butter into a batter. Leave to rest for 10 minutes.

Heat the oil or ghee in a non-stick frying pan and drop small tablespoons of batter into the pan, keeping them separate. Fry over a moderate heat for about 1 minute on each side, until golden on both sides. Drain the biscuits on a plate lined with kitchen paper. They are best served straightaway while still warm, crisp on the edges and chewy on the inside.

80g plain flour
70g caster sugar
2 tbsp skimmed milk powder
140ml milk
1 brown cardamom pod, seeds
   removed and pounded in a
   pestle and mortar
1½ tsp fennel seeds, ground
pinch of salt
1 tbsp ground almonds
2 tbsp melted butter
4 tbsp ghee or vegetable oil,
   for frying

GLOSSARY

As well as the more familiar English translations for ingredients, I've also given the Indian names which you may come across in Indian stores.

SPICES

Asafoetida (heeng)

A really pungent powder that helps digestion and as such is added to many dishes that are hard to digest. Use the smallest pinch as it is very strong. If you don't have any, leave it out – it won't affect the dish too much.

Black/brown cardamom pods (badi elaichi)

These large woody pods look as though they are well past their sell-by date but have a wonderful and strong flavour when cooked. They are an important element in garam masala and pilaffs.

Black peppercorns (kali mirch)

Little needs to be said here, except that the taste and aroma of freshly ground peppercorns is far superior to store-bought powder.

Brown mustard seeds (rai)

These brown seeds are used a lot in India. It is to the south what cumin is to the north. It is also a key element in pickle making. When added to hot oil, the seeds will splutter, so it is good to have a cover handy to stop them popping out of the pan. Once cooked, they become almost nutty. When ground into a powder they provide a tart note to dishes and when ground into a paste they are the very essence of mustard.

Carom seeds/bishops weed (ajwain)

A small dark green seed that is reminiscent of thyme. It is quite strong so you only ever need to use a little. We often use it with fish and in some Indian breads. It is also an instantaneous cure for a stomach ache. Take half a teaspoonful with a pinch of salt and drink with hot water.

Chaat masala

A blend of spices that few Indians make at home. It is spicy and tart and Indians sprinkle it over many cooked foods and even drinks for a kick of flavour.

Cinnamon/cassia bark (dal chini)

Cassia bark is used more than cinnamon in India and has a smoother flavour. Use either sparingly as it has a big flavour and can overpower others. I add it in shards – any more and it will be too much.

Cloves (laung)

A strong spice that is most commonly used in garam masala. The natural oil in this is great for a toothache – bite down on the clove where it hurts and hold it there for as long as possible.

Coriander seeds and powder (sabut dhaniya)

Coriander seeds come from the flowers of the coriander plant. They are wonderfully mild and aromatic and are abundantly used. They have a subtle flavour but once you know what they taste like, you can always identify their presence. I often drink a coriander-seed tea after meals as it helps digestion and is cooling on the body. The seeds, when powdered, are used as a base for many masalas and it is probably the most used spice in my kitchen. Good-quality store-bought powder will be mossy green rather than brown.

Cumin seeds (jira)

This familiar spice is earthy when cooked in oil and nutty when dry roasted. It is an important spice in our cooking and adds a lovely rounded flavour. Great for digestion when made into a light warm tea.

Dried mango powder (amchur)

This ingredient is actually made from dried raw mangoes. It is tangy and we often sprinkle it on to cooked tandoori foods or fried potatoes instead of lemon juice or vinegar. It doesn't need cooking.

Fennel seeds/aniseeds (saunf)

A sweet, liquorice-like spice. They are often seen in the cuisine of Kashmir but also in the south. They are good for the stomach, and cooling and great for breast-feeding

when infused in hot water. Also a natural breath freshener – chew on a few after a meal.

Fenugreek seeds (methi)

Strong, bitter seeds that have that familiar 'curry' flavour. Use very little at any time.

Garam masala

This famous blend is at its purest composed of the strong flavours of cloves, black cardamom, cinnamon and green cardamom. We add bay leaves, mace and black peppercorn to this. Many milder brands will add coriander and cumin seeds. This powder can be added towards the end of cooking for a real punch of aroma or closer to the beginning for a more rounded, subtle taste.

Green cardamom pod (chotti elaichi)

This is one of my favourite spices. It has a soft but powerful aroma and is used in sweet and savoury dishes and is essential in spicy tea. The seeds can be ground to make green cardamom powder.

Mace (javitri)

A wonderful flavour which goes very well with meat and chicken.

Nigella seeds (kalonji)

These delicate black seeds have a peppery flavour but without the bite.

Red chilli powder (lal mirch)

This is usually very hot and adds great colour to a dish but not much flavour.

Saffron (kesa)

Saffron is the dried stamen of the crocus flower. It is very expensive but a little goes a long way and it keeps well in the fridge. A lovely, musky flavour that works in both savoury and sweet dishes. Try to find long stamens.

Turmeric powder (haldi)

This vibrant powder is essential in Indian

cooking. It is prized for its colour and its fantastic medicinal properties.

White poppy seeds (khus khus)

These are the same as the familiar dark poppy seeds but without the black husk. The skinless seeds have a smoother character then their dark cousins.

LENTILS

Bengal gram (channa dal)

The whole bean is similar to the chickpea but smaller and with a dark-brown skin. Once skinned and split, the bean becomes a wonderful, earthy, yellow lentil.

Split and skinned black gram (urad dal)

This small, delicate lentil is used a lot in south Indian food for texture as it is sautéed to a nutty crunch without being pre-boiled.

Split and skinned mung bean (dhuli mung ki dal)

This small, pale yellow lentil is one of the easiest to digest and has a subtle, buttery flavour. At home, this is the lentil we eat most.

Split yellow pigeon pea lentil (toovar/arhar dal)

This lentil is often cooked until it completely breaks down to a smooth paste and is then spiced before being served. Wash well as it is usually coated in a film of oil to help preserve it.

FLOURS

Chapatti flour

A blend of wholewheat and plain flour that is used to make our most common flatbreads. It can be found in Indian stores as well as many of the larger supermarkets. Substitute with equal quantities of plain and wholewheat flour.

Gram flour (besan)

A key ingredient in Indian cookery and made from powdered Bengal gram. The Northern Indians use it to make batters, to bind marinades in tandoori foods, to flavour vegetables and also to make simple wheat-free breads. It has more protein than wheat. It can now be found in large supermarkets.

Rice flour

In India rice flour would be made by soaking the grains, drying them in the sun and then grinding them to a fine powder. This is used to add crispness to fried foods, to make dumplings in the south, to thicken curries and in the north to make a ground rice pudding. A delicate and fragrant flour that I love and use it as a thickener instead of cornflour.

OTHERS

Buttermilk

A by-product of the butter-making process. It may seem like a tangy version of skimmed milk but, once flavoured, it is absolutely delicious and easier to digest than milk or yoghurt.

Curry leaves (kari patta)

These leaves are truly fragrant. They add a taste of the south to any dish they are added to.

Ghee (clarified butter)

Prized for its medicinal qualities in the East. It has a strong aroma and burns at a higher temperature than butter. See also page 12.

Jaggery (gur)

This is a completely unrefined sugar and probably the healthiest sugar around. It is made by boiling the natural sap from the date palm until it is hard and sets in a block. It is full of minerals and has a host of healthy properties. Workers in dusty Delhi factories are given little nuggets of jaggery to help keep their lungs clean. Buy

the darkest you can find as they are less watery and have a more defined flavour.

Paneer

This traditional Indian cheese is made without rennet or bacterial culture (see page 27). It is similar to fresh farmer's cheese and looks like solid ricotta. I think it is fabulous and is an important source of protein for Indian vegetarians.

Pilaff

A term used for any spiced and seasoned rice dish. It can be simple or contain any number of added ingredients.

Raita

A term used for yoghurt once it has had ingredients added to it. You can add cooked or raw, crunchy vegetables or even fruit to it. A wonderful summery dish that is great with any barbecues as well as full-on Indian meals.

Tamarind (imli)

The tamarind tree bears wonderful pods of fruit which are thick, fibrous and full of large seeds. But once softened and strained, the tamarind paste is a wonderful, tangy ingredient. It has a fruity, sour flavour and is used prolifically in the south, often to balance the sweetness of the coconut in their curries. The ready-made paste is available in the market but they all differ in strength so add to taste.

Tandoori cooking

A tandoor is a barrel-shaped clay oven and is so popular it is now used all over the world. The temperature in a tandoor can reach 500°F and gives dishes a barbecue-like flavour by searing it on the outside.

INDEX

WRITING A BOOK IS ALWAYS A PRODUCTION. Like an Indian wedding, it involves many key people without whom it wouldn't have been possible. I want to thank my husband for always believing in me and everything I do. To my sister, for always being so supportive and so generous with her time, filling in any gaps of loneliness in my daughter's life. To Heather, for being such a fantastic agent and ambassador. To Elly, for being so helpful and calm during the many periods of madness. To the powers-that-be in the BBC for giving me this fantastic opportunity and for such a wonderful experience. And last, but by no means least, to the team at Quadrille for succeeding so effortlessly in putting together this beautiful book in record time.